HOW TO READ FOR FUN

HOW to READ for FUN

JAMIE KIM

LUMINARE PRESS
WWW.LUMINAREPRESS.COM

How to Read for Fun
Copyright ©2022 by Jamie Kim

All rights reserved. This book or any portion thereof may not be reproduced or used in any manner whatsoever without the express written permission of the publisher, except for the use of brief quotations in a book review.

Printed in the United States of America

Luminare Press
442 Charnelton St.
Eugene, OR 97401
www.luminarepress.com

LCCN: 2022915708
ISBN: 979-8-88679-084-9

To Mom and Dad

CONTENTS

Preface ix

Understanding Why 1
How to Separate *Ugh* Reading
from Reading 21
The Approach 35
Making Time 52
Finding Good Books 66
Romanticization 85

Referenced Literature 97
Resources 108
Acknowledgments 111

Preface

Dear Reader,

I know I'm trying to get you to like reading by reading, which we both know you don't really enjoy if you're here. It's fair. You don't have time, you don't know what to read, you don't read fast enough, it's too nerdy, it's boring—the list goes on. But before you give up on your chances of being someone who reads for fun, hear me out (this book isn't long, I promise). I want to take this opportunity and show you why reading really isn't that bad. In fact, it can be *fun*. If we're lucky, you might even want to go out and find *that book*: the one that you just can't put down. After you've done that? Sorry. You'll officially be a convert.

    Unfortunately, not everyone pops out of the womb ready to read Tolstoy. You've probably read up on the benefits of literature (or maybe some well-meaning friend or parent has made *sure* you know why you should read). Yet despite what everyone says, including me, it isn't that easy. I'm not writing this to force you to read more—no one has time for that. Reading for fun is a tool that makes your life easier if you know how to do it right. And that's what this book is here for.

I know you might be reluctant to take advice, much less "help," from a teenager. I promise that my age won't affect the importance or validity of anything I tell you. I've been a reader my whole life, so I've experienced its benefits firsthand, but that also means that I know precisely how difficult it is to choose to read with so many other things on your plate. I also know how difficult it might feel to get started. Reading *can* be enjoyable, and we can turn it into something you'll grow to love. This book will tell you everything you need to know. Before you know it, you'll be reading for fun too.

Good luck,
Jamie

Turn to the "**Referenced Literature**" section at the back of this book for more information on the titles mentioned in the following chapters.

CHAPTER 1

Understanding Why

WHO READS FOR FUN, MUCH LESS WRITES AN entire book about it? In the face of a world that prioritizes convenience and speed over all, the art of reading is dying. The vast majority of peers you ask will tell you that they find reading boring, or that reading for fun is "impossible." Telling someone you like to read will, more likely than not, get you a raised eyebrow, a disbelieving smile, or sometimes a rare expression of envy. Why would anyone *choose* to read at all?

The first step to learning anything new is understanding why you're doing it. How many times have we been taught to do something that is useless in the context of reality? Reading for fun isn't like your average trigonometry homework: it's useful in real life, actually engaging, and it'll be of real worth to you in every context. When you hit those first couple bumps in the road after you start reading on your own time, if the reason why you're doing what you're doing is not clear, it'll be all too easy to lose motivation, save it for another day, or give up. In this chapter, we'll talk about defining a purpose and review the most significant impacts of consistent reading. Before learning the *how*, you'll need to understand your *why*.

PERSPECTIVE

There are countless statistics, facts, articles, lectures, seminars—even classes you can go to in hopes of learning the merits of reading. I won't bog you down by repeating all of them (although most of the things they say are true). It's likely you've already been told many times why reading is good for you. Teachers, family, maybe you even have a reader friend who begs you, every so often, to check out a particularly amazing book they've come across lately. Despite how many times you've told them no, have you ever really considered why not? Is it a lack of time? Does it feel like work? Is it too nerdy? Is it boring? Do you have better things to do?

While most read for fun simply because they find it entertaining, the fact that you've picked up this book means you're making a conscious effort to choose literature as your medium of choice. Why? You could just as easily have opened YouTube and watched videos of luxury cars or switched on the TV and caught last week's airing of *Saturday Night Live*. There's something about a book, as compared to a show or a video game, that makes it more meaningful than the average diversion.

And since we're at it anyway, why not attach a deeper meaning to it? Reading for fun should be, by definition, fun. But it is so much more, and even if you don't recognize it as it happens, your mind subconsciously absorbs literature's incredible benefits. Reading is proven to make your life easier, even if it may not feel that way at first. Whether it be in regards to school, relationships, or future plans, you might be surprised by the extent to which little things can become simpler and faster. Once you truly embark on your reading journey, other parts of your life will naturally become more enjoyable.

Every impact that reading will impart on you is a personal one. These impacts might eventually affect your surroundings or relationships, but everything you learn from what you read goes through *you*. This is why literature is so powerful—it's a transformative experience that lasts long after you've turned the last page.

...

Before the internet was created, 'media' meant 'print'. People used it to teach, spread news, write stories… actually, practically every revolution in the eighteenth century involved a piece of writing that was instrumental in inflaming the people. It's hard to imagine any piece of literature being that unifying in modern times, but the fact is that written literature can be capable of as much power as you choose to give it. You might not even realize it as it happens, but each story can transport your mind to the far corners of the globe or even beyond this universe, all from the comfort of your room.

Once you learn to consume a book—appreciatively—it'll not only open your eyes to the world the author has painted for you but also facets of the real world you may have missed before. Every author writes differently. I like to think that each work we read gives us a "dimension"—something like a combination of perspective and proportion in the author's eyes. The more you read, the more dimensions you'll be introduced to. Some will be completely foreign, while others might be eerily familiar.

For example, take the concept of New York. To me, as someone who was born and raised in Colorado, New York is a fascinating metropolis characterized by aggressive car horns, Wall Street, and heavily-accented, bizarre population. *The Great Gatsby* paints the region as a booming party scene that helps a man reunite with his one true love. But the way that *Catcher in the Rye* tells it, New York is a representation of everything to be despised in life—a city that repeatedly smacks our narrator in the face with the reminder of his loneliness. And in *The Other Wes Moore*, we learn that New York can be a clear-cut demonstration of the sharp inequity in America but also a vibrant center of cultural mingling and coexistence. The important thing to remember is that behind every character is an author with their own experiences, opinions, and desires. New York is an easy target—everyone writes about New York. But the same dimensions are applicable to anything you might read, whether it be a news story, opinion article, or novel.

And to the point of perception: many of you have likely thought that people who read for fun are nerds. Geeks. Or just plain weird. I've heard them all—directed at other people, at myself, and surprisingly most often by readers to themselves. We can't blame people for thinking this way, because a lot of us have been trained since childhood to associate a book with social awkwardness. Reading for fun might be tainted with its association of "nerdiness." But in truth, this connotation means nothing unless you choose to let it mean more. In a perfect world, being a 'reader' would feel like a badge of honor.

Who hasn't seen a movie that has the token nerd character? (Cough, *Princess Diaries*?) She's likely got thick glasses, frizzy hair, and wears patterned knee-high socks with plaid skirts, but more importantly, she's always got a book in hand. And yet—once that physical stereotype goes away, either by makeover or age or some other miracle, the unattractive characteristic of loving to read becomes an attribute.

Take Hermione Granger, J. K. Rowling's fierce heroine from the *Harry Potter* novels. In both books and movies, Hermione begins her first few years at Hogwarts teased for her bushy hair and buck teeth, despite her ferocious determination and intelligence. She's known for always having her nose in a book and her inability to resist raising her hand in class. Apart from her best friends Harry and Ron, she's largely rejected from the general community at school. Starting in the fourth book (*Harry Potter and the Goblet of Fire*) though, age and adventures begin to diffuse these physical features, and she's portrayed as quite pretty. She dates a Quidditch celebrity, takes whoever she wants to Christmas parties, and begins making several friends outside of her trio. All the while, her bookish qualities remain present and outstanding.

Liking reading is only an off-putting quality if you make it so. Hermione's less-charming years might have included her book-worminess, but they were not defined by it. Similarly, reading for fun will not magic you into a nerd unless you wish it to. So don't spare a thought toward people's perception of you as a reader. Frankly, they won't care, and you'll still be you.

Take this opportunity to consider the possibility that the millions of books in our world allow. Being able to read for fun opens a billion doors—and each of them can transform the way you think, feel, and act. Allow yourself to step into a new perspective and embrace all that reading for fun has to offer.

CONNECTION

When you picture reading, you probably aren't thinking of it as a group activity. Sitting holed up somewhere, nose buried in a book…not really the recipe for a social butterfly, is it? Despite this instinctual connotation, reading can actually improve your social skills. Somewhere between the lines of each page lies a heightened sense of empathy, compassion, and interpersonal connection.

Reading is a tool that helps you understand multiple perspectives like no other. Each story, regardless of genre, takes you to a completely different life. Whether it be memoir, fantasy, science fiction…you can adopt a different name, live in a different country (or universe), believe in a different religion, or step out of the skin of a human entirely. Each time you dive into a new author's words, you let go of who you are and begin to look differently—see differently. Once you've finished with the words, that new perspective doesn't leave you.

Just by opening a cover, you can bask in the cheers of hundreds of thousands who have tuned in to watch you win the international championships. You can fall deep, deep in love as a city thrums around you—or brave an apocalypse. You can don an astronaut's helmet and feel the exhilarating terror of exploring space as you listen to the crackle of the radio and your own harsh breathing. You can sit in on meetings as rich men and women make decisions that will ripple across the globe. You can feel the bone-deep hunger of a starving child and watch as he licks his fingers for sustenance. You can experience the bombing of Hiroshima from the eyes of a survivor.

To read is not to simply look at ink deliberately placed on paper—it is to understand the world we live in. Sometimes the knowledge is passed on directly, in an objective analysis, but other times we have to search, dive through layers, to find an author's intent. Through their words, and that search, we learn to feel for others. We begin to understand why some may act as they do, and we start to realize that no matter how long we search, we'll never truly be able to understand everything. Suddenly others' acts of calculation, passion, desperation make more sense. Everything that people do is justified to themselves, and even when reading cannot provide that justification, it reminds us that it's there.

In "The Case for Reading Fiction" in the June 2020 *Harvard Business Review,* Christine Seifert discusses how "reading fiction predicts increased social acuity and a sharper ability to comprehend other people's motivations…Characters, plots, and settings in foreign locales help anchor difficult discussions. The narrative allows participants to work through sensitive and nuanced issues in an open and honest manner." This effect teaches us to subconsciously mirror such candor in our independent lives. Becoming more empathetic and open doesn't only make you a better person within—others will see it too. Reading's impacts will start to become apparent in the way you maintain your relationships. How do you handle your connections? Suddenly, reading a story of another's struggle has made you more receptive to those of your family and friends.

...

The use of language is practically universal—and this means that reading can enhance your ability to form connections with others. A person's perspective on literature can speak volumes about themselves. First, do they read at all? What do they read? How do they read? Where do they read? What's their favorite genre? Favorite book? Telling someone that your favorite book is *Twilight* will leave a drastically different impression than saying it's *The 48 Laws of Power*. The impression your reading leaves on others can have important outcomes. For example, one of the questions this year's applicants to Columbia University were asked was: "list the titles of the books, essays, poetry, short stories, or plays you read outside of academic courses that you enjoyed most during secondary/high school." The primary purpose of such questions is for admissions officers to get a sense of who you are—that's how much your taste in literature can help decipher you as a person.

There's something magical about the way reading, among other things, can tie people together. Even when one of the parties hasn't read the book yet, recommending a novel—as compared to a show or movie—feels more consequential. Because books are so dynamic, reading one at the request of another person shows a willingness to bridge boundaries and get to know their ideas better. Telling someone you actually went back and read something they recommended to you demonstrates a great deal of effort and can earn you their instant respect. You can spend an afternoon binge-watching a show a friend suggested, but reading their favorite book shows much more dedication (even if you'd enjoy both activities the same amount).

Plus, having at least a foundational knowledge of the literary world is a powerful tool in certain circles of society, and simple conversation about any book can help you effortlessly gain good standing with a new acquaintance. You'll also catch more allusions to commonly known stories scattered throughout other media and dialogue. Randomly stumbling across someone who shares a passion for reading is rare, but cherished.

There are annotated texts, book clubs, reading seminars, literary documentaries, and (my favorite) movies based on books that all allow you to experience the same text from a different person's point of view. There are even speakeasies reserved solely for "literary-minded people". Reading itself might be a solitary activity, but it can also act as your ticket to priceless experiences and communities. Particularly popular novels have entire fandoms—fan theory, art, discussion, and fanfiction all centered around a single story.

This might all feel way out of your depth. To someone who's never voluntarily touched a book before, of course the idea of creating bonds with real people through reading might feel overwhelming. Don't worry. No one's going to come up and pelt you with questions like, "What was the main plot device of *In Cold Blood*?" You may never end up discussing books with other readers, by choice or by chance. Either way, there are endless possibilities that your decision to read for fun opens. They are options that are always there to take, but only if you want them, so don't let them burden you.

EDUCATION

Say you're not really into the whole "finding a literary community" thing. What else makes reading so important? Turns out, our teachers were right about this one. As unlikely as it might seem, spending some consistent time reading for fun can make key parts of your life much easier—and that includes school.

A huge part of reading successfully within constrained time (for assignments, AP tests, projects, finals, etc.) depends on your reading speed. Your "words processed per minute," or WPM, is a tangible measure of the rate at which you read. We've all heard that practice makes perfect, and studies show that the more you read, the faster you read. This means that consistent interpretation of written literature can significantly increase your WPM.

This faster reading pace not only allows you to get through stories quicker but also optimizes your ability to read for due dates and deadlines. The three assigned chapters that were due on Friday might have once taken you an entire afternoon to get through, but not anymore.

Why can't you just read more work material to increase your WPM? You always can, but time tends to pass much faster and far more enjoyably when you're reading something that genuinely engages you. Would you rather spend half an hour after lunch reading scientific journal articles or *The Hunger Games*? A good author will paint their world for you, introduce you to characters, and take you on adventures. All you have to do is sit back, relax, and enjoy the ride. You can grow a tail and dance with mermaids, fall in love with a mysterious neighbor, or even crawl around war zones. Meanwhile, your brain will begin to store the innumerable benefits literature has to offer. All you have to do is open a page and look at it.

Approaching reading with the mindset that it can be enjoyable is the key to actually making it feel that way. If it helps, you can think of the books you read for pleasure as practice for the reading you'll have to complete as work. An increased reading speed makes the task shorter, while your improved relationship with literature in general can alleviate a lot of the displeasure you might feel right now about the words "assigned reading."

Reading material that you don't come across in your everyday routine also expands your exposure to vocabulary and writing style. Even if the literature you've come across isn't enjoyable, as Stephen King puts it in his book, *On Writing*: "One learns most clearly what not to do by reading bad prose." Exposing yourself to what other authors have written will make you a faster and more eloquent writer. Although it's not exactly a skill you can put on your resume, improved writing ability can help you manage your professional and educational life to its maximum efficiency.

Common assignments like literary analysis, research projects, and essays will become far easier with time. Consistent reading doesn't only increase your capacity to consume literature, it helps you understand it, too. Reading is useless if not for comprehension, and while you're reading for fun, you'll be so invested in the story that the comprehension will come unconsciously—after all, the author's goal is to keep you eager for what happens next.

Time starts to fly by as you learn to read for fun, and you'll start to pick up these skills without additional effort. When you take those skills and apply them to reading that really isn't fun, they'll still hold. This means that your increased WPM will get you through it faster, your improved comprehension will prevent you from having to go back and repeat sections, and you'll be able to draw more meaning from the text. In no time, work readings will feel less like a monstrosity and more like busywork that you can easily glide through.

A faster reading pace combined with an expanded vocabulary and writing expertise can also naturally help you excel in tests, particularly standardized tests like the SAT and ACT. Such tests are specifically built to measure skills that can be subconsciously gained from consistent reading. You'll be less pressed for time because you read faster, comprehend faster, and analyze faster. As a result, studying for the reading or English sections on standardized tests won't be nearly as difficult—answering those types of questions will feel almost instinctual.

We haven't even touched on what can be learned from the content of the literature itself yet. Apart from the skill growth, the perspective change, and the mental shift, reading imparts an enormous amount of knowledge in a depth that is nearly impossible to achieve by any other medium. Writing itself is a lasting record of knowledge and perspective, and the length and physical density of the typical book allows for optimized detail and accuracy. Informational books are essentially online articles on steroids.

Reading something, as compared to watching a video or hearing about it in passing, can deliver vast amounts of information on any chosen topic. Depending on what you opt to read, you can learn about anything, from the history of the human species (*Sapiens: A Brief History of Humankind*) to the best vinegar to use in orange chicken (*The Modern Proper Cookbook*).

This brings us back to the classroom. In almost any class, a pre-existing knowledge base in the subject at hand makes the course itself easier, more comprehensible, and more interesting. Some classes like AP Language & Composition and most every AP history class will have you write free-response questions, where bringing in outside knowledge is not only recommended but necessary to score well. Context is often crucial to understanding, and consistent reading is one of the best ways to arm yourself with background knowledge.

And it's always nice to know more. Growing your knowledge base makes you not only smarter but also more interesting—you'll always have something intriguing to say, and eventually you'll start making tons of connections to random things in daily life. Reading fills your mind with new facts, new information, and new ideas. Not bad for a cover-bound stack of paper, right?

MENTAL HEALTH

Learning to read for fun goes far beyond connections and test scores. It allows the whole world to melt away. Any struggles, anxieties, fears, or sadness you're dealing with might still be there when you return, but you can forget them for a little while as you adopt a different character's world. It's like handing yourself a "Get Out of Jail Free" card from life. Any conflicts in the plot that you're reading about? We know they'll be solved eventually (although not always with a happy ending, we know we'll get closure regardless). With some types of reading (particularly feel-good, rom com, comedy, etc.) there's that inherent trust that everything will eventually turn out okay—nothing will end in complete devastation because there will always be another part to the story. Leaving life's unknowns and allowing yourself to be pulled into that trust can help your mind learn to relax, hope, and heal.

On the flip side, there are also works of literature that provide comfort in a different way. There are just as many stories that end in sorrow, tragedy, or even the main character's demise as there are stories that boast of a happy ending. Just like you can pull yourself into a better world through reading, you can also put your life into a different light by juxtaposing it with a worse one. It's up to you to curate your own emotional reading experience in a way that makes sense to you. You won't always be able to control everything that happens to you in "real life," but reading gives you the power to select content in line with what you want to feel.

Setting aside time for reading can also help you build structure, and therefore stability, in each day. It'll become a rhythm, a dynamic constant that will always be there for you no matter how great or awful the day has gone. The repetitive act of reading makes it a uniquely comforting activity for many. This aspect of reading can also improve the quality of your sleep and make it easier to fall asleep quickly. A lot of people also choose to read right before bed because it's been shown to reduce stress, prime your body for good sleep, and allow for mental relaxation. Think of it like washing the whole day away by entering a different one.

Written stories have the ability to make real life seem inconsequential, a quality that can feel oddly comforting. It's a form of escapism—any time this world becomes too much, you can run away and hide for a while in a different one. Reading can also provide a certain reassurance that no matter how we're feeling, we're always given the option to live these characters' lives. They also often endure similar or far worse than we do and emerge successful, or at least grow from their experiences. It can be inspirational, in a way.

A couple years ago, I read *World War Z* by Max Brooks—a book that speaks of a world of survival, disaster, and regrowth after the Zombie War (essentially a global zombie apocalypse). But the story isn't told like a typical narrative. Readers visit short stories of different survivors of different class, age, and status across the globe, piecing together the story of humanity's survival.

Years after I'd finished the book without thinking too much of it, *World War Z* kept strangely coming to mind. We'd all had a terrible few months—COVID had swept through everyone's lives (this was during the initial global lockdown), everything had been upended, and I was very, very deep in my head. During that time, I couldn't let go of the idea of this book and that something so oddly similar, yet drastically different, could have been shaped through someone else's mind and written decades before. The cause of the zombie apocalypse in this novel was essentially a virus that also originated in China, and the institutional and political responses to the book's disaster and real life's disaster, COVID, were crazily reminiscent of each other. In the swirling chaos of both timelines, I found a peculiar reassurance. At least as our world went down the drain, I knew this other world had gone through it, too.

World War Z didn't mean too much to me when I first read it. Sure, it was always a great book—gripping, eerie, and fascinating—but when the pandemic hit it became something else entirely. The book was almost like a guide to the worst-case scenario, and it told me I should be grateful that at least we weren't enduring the aftermath of a whole zombie war (although at times it did feel a little like it). But Brooks's words were also a reminder. There is no need to worry about things you can't control, and if you can't remind yourself of that, then find something else to remind you. Even if that something else ends up being a work of fiction.

No experience with any single novel is the same, but the lasting impact literature can leave on its audience is indisputable. Whether you use reading as an escape or a reassurance, it will offer you a different view on the lives we lead. Sometimes being forced to step back and reassess is all we need to feel a little better.

And don't forget about literature that was specifically intended to improve mental health. There are thousands of books out there targeted solely towards life improvement, emotional security, and the achievement of happiness, all of which can help you attain such goals. Reading can help us appreciate the privileges we receive, motivate us to grow further, and prime our minds for relaxation. It's certainly not a cure-all, but it has the ability to change our mindsets and, in the end, our mental health.

...

As you start to read for leisure, keep all of these reasons in mind. What stood out to you the most? What are you aiming to achieve through your reading? And if you're just here to have fun, these incredible benefits might keep you going in times when literature might not seem so engaging. Through perception, connection, skill development, and comfort, reading has the power to change your life for the better. Always keep your *why* in mind.

CHAPTER 2

How to Separate
Ugh Reading from Reading

SOMETIMES IT FEELS IMPOSSIBLE TO READ IN a way that doesn't make you feel like you should be clocked in. The second step to reading for fun is differentiating it from work. Assignments, required readings, any kind of reading you're forced to do? Writing that makes you want to groan, or sleep, or stuff your head under a pillow? That's *ugh* reading. It's a real thing, and even those that already read for leisure can often find it dreary. As readers, we want to separate *ugh* reading from *reading*, the kind of reading that we want to be doing. *Reading* is optional, engaging, and most importantly, fun.

In this chapter, we'll make that key differentiation between *reading* and *ugh* reading, then learn how to get past the *ugh* kind of literature. We'll talk about why it's so easy to dislike certain writings, how to determine whether a particular book was meant for you, and how to *enjoy* reading, for real. I'm hoping that it'll be enough for you to give reading another chance.

UGH READING'S ROOTS

I was told by my first, second, and third-grade teachers to try and read for at least twenty minutes every night. They'd even send out emails to our parents, ensuring that those of us with unyielding guardians would be sat down in a chair daily and be forced to pretend to read for at least those twenty minutes (I remember that my mom, in her ever well-meaning harshness, stretched that number to a dreaded thirty). For those who did not have that external pressure, there was no incentive to read in the first place. How many children are angelic enough to do something in their own time just because their teacher said to? This approach to developing an affinity for literature from a young age was at times successful, but mostly it did nothing but backfire. Telling kids that there is something they should do, then proceeding to treat it as a requirement, is a recipe for resentment.

How many of us actually did read for those twenty minutes? I, for one, know I skimmed through about a chapter in two minutes or so before zoning out at the wall and daydreaming for the remaining time. It was either that or fidgeting with my hands and eyeing the clock every few seconds—I was less willing to read during that half-hour than I was at *any* other time of day. As soon as that timer ended, my reading for the day was finally complete. Heads up. Books down. Brush off your hands and stretch your backs, everyone; it's time to play! The later years of school have continued to reinforce the misguided idea of reading as a "twenty minutes every night" sort of thing, and it has caused a generational hostility towards leisure reading.

Even unconsciously, there's also that lasting impression that literature can only exist while tied to school and school only. Putting a quantifiable time count on reading might have been intended to foster a youthful passion for reading, but schools (and yes, parents too) went about it the wrong way. There are even bookmarks sold at school book fairs with tiny stopwatches on them. I mean, how's a kid supposed to grow a love for reading if they're being trained to think of it as a chore? Being forced to do anything, especially at such a young age, makes whatever it is, regardless of what it entails, become work. Fold your laundry, finish your homework, set the table, do your reading…they're bound to blend together.

The construction of *ugh* reading doesn't stop in primary school. Just like our educational system, tying reading to a negative, repetitive, forced activity won't get you anywhere. This is maybe you, or maybe someone you know—you go to school one day and come home with a beaten-up-looking book in hand and instructions to read until page 34. That drab little collection of pages is going to sit abandoned either on your kitchen island or in the depths of your backpack for the seven days until the assignment is due. When the due date comes, you'll take out the book just to mark its title, skim the novel's SparkNotes on Google, trudge off to class, and ace your quiz.

There's a lot wrong with this situation and the fact that it's happened to practically anyone who's been in high school in the past decade or so, but I won't get into all that. You were able to succeed by merely reading SparkNotes, CliffsNotes, or any other summary instead of the passage you should have read. In your perspective, this saved you time, effort, and boredom while attaining the same score. Because of this, teachers have unwittingly conditioned us to feel that reading in general is not "worth" it, and that reading for enjoyment is out of the question. I mean, why read a novel for fun when you could watch the trailer of its movie adaptation instead, right? This pattern of misguided approach to assigned reading has roots that stretch all the way back to elementary school, and it's compounded on a certain mindset that there are far more convenient ways to absorb the information that reading a book would give you.

Essentially, we've been trained wrong. Beyond childhood, our secondary and higher education years often only succeed in solidifying a distaste for reading. High school teachers (and perhaps professors too) often attempt to dissect literature and find deeper meaning when there often isn't intended to be one. It's because the idea of teaching values through reading has become widely normalized, despite its blatant flaws. Authors' intended meanings are often supplanted by a jury of readers and teachers, and every reader interprets themes in novels differently. Answering a worksheet question like, "What did the coin symbolize?" doesn't make for moral learning, much less a passion for literature. To put this into context, how many of us were taught about racism through *To Kill a Mockingbird*? Nevermind that the novel, which is used in classrooms nationwide to teach about prejudice, was written by a white woman in the late 1950's.

By taking this so-called "educational approach," we've learned to loathe novels that are meant to be *read*, not flayed and scrutinized. The type of novels we read in a typical American English class are often engaging to the right reader under the right circumstances. But when the words are rubbed in our faces, lessons wrung from pages long since bled dry? Of course the stories often fall flat. "I Know Why the Caged Bird Cannot Read" by Francine Prose is a great essay that details the exact relationship between the American education system and our generational distaste for literature. The piece evidences how schools are twisting common book-list titles—including *Nineteen Eighty-four*, *Of Mice and Men*, and *Lord of the Flies*—into more than they are, with often unintended consequences. Trying to pry out social justice and controversial issues from books not intended for that purpose has often tainted students with a lack of enthusiasm for such reading.

What all of this means for us is that anything negative you've thought, learned, or been taught about reading from the educational system, or really any institution, is completely justified. But it should also be chucked out the window as you approach reading for fun. We don't want a literary analysis or a ten page write-up; we're not going to be squeezing unintended moral lessons from our books. If a theme jumps out at you, makes you *feel* something? That's good. That's right. But for now, take the bad taste that reading for school has left on your tongue and try to ignore it. Eventually you'll encounter books that interest, engage, and captivate you. When you do, allow yourself to approach the idea of reading for fun with an open mind as it retrains you to genuinely appreciate written language.

And stay strong, because once you're out of school, *ugh* reading doesn't go away. Any professional work you might be doing often requires research and extensive reading for several different contexts. Hypothetically, let's consider Julie. Julie's recently graduated from college and she's been granted the opportunity to intern for a notable nearby law firm. Exhilarated, she accepts the offer, knowing it'll be a strenuous experience but worth it. Quickly, she finds herself drowning in documents: transcripts, reports, research articles… some may enjoy the reading they come across in their line of work, but to Julie these dull pages become a significant drag to her days at the firm.

One afternoon, Julie's friend Caitlin calls her up. Caitlin's always been a passionate reader and is a particular fan of poetry. She's called Julie to tell her about the latest poetry book she's come across—a collection so good it'd be a crime to miss out on. Julie tries to picture it: a colorful cover that houses lines and lines of creative verse. Unbidden, though, her mind scrambles to shift that image into the paper-clipped stack of papers she was supposed to read through by Tuesday night. Unable to imagine enjoying such literature, Julie dejectedly tells Caitlin she'll look into the book later, knowing she won't get to it.

Don't let yourself become Julie. Had she taken Caitlin up on her offer, Julie might have found that the poetry book was in fact enjoyable, and that she could read one short poem before bed each night. If Julie had not allowed her experience with work reading to interfere, she might have discovered a hidden interest in other prose and found that her research sometimes resembled the stories she read for pleasure.

At some point in your career, reading might come to consist solely of ledgers or scientific journals, or whatever you encounter at work. But don't let it taint your view of literature as a whole. It's important to always make a clear distinction between necessity and choice: is what you have in front of you *ugh* reading or *reading*?.

Even if these scenarios aren't something you've personally experienced, they may remind you that any prior experiences with literature and the situations you've been conditioned by (or might be conditioned by in the future) should not be a measure of your ability to read for enjoyment. While it is understandably difficult to simply erase all unpleasant memories and experiences you've associated with reading thus far, try not to let it affect your willingness to try again. There is literature that better suits you out there, and there are better ways to *read* that literature.

ARE YOU THE AUDIENCE?

I love reading. I'm even writing a book about it. And yet I still despise the majority of readings I've been assigned—in school and out. Even considering the misteaching we've already talked about… It's just *boring*. But that's fine because I know it's *ugh* reading. The uncontrollable distaste I feel when I look at *Beowulf* won't affect the excitement *The Hunger Games* can induce. *Reading*, real reading, isn't intended to put you to sleep. In fact, the number one goal of modern authors is to engage their audience. If ancient poems or historical fiction are your vibe, go for it. But a large part of the separation from work and fun reading is the content of the literature itself. So, if those genres bore you to death? We'll work on finding a better match.

Unfortunately, you won't get anywhere if you're trying to read an *ugh* piece of literature for your pleasure reading. Now, *ugh* is defined a little differently for everyone. One of my dearest friends has the strangest love for true crime books, but I absolutely cannot stand them. To me, *Zodiac* by Robert Graysmith sounds like many fearful, sleepless nights. But her? She'd blow through the novel in a single afternoon. Remember that a book that was an incredible experience for someone else might very possibly be completely unenjoyable to you, and that says much more about your reading *taste* than your ability to read for leisure. Stay aware of *what* it is that you're reading, and remind yourself that if it's not required, you might as well spend your time on reading you enjoy.

This is the main difference between *ugh* reading and fun reading. *Ugh* reading will fall outside your range of interest—if that kind of literature is all that you've been exposed to thus far, no wonder you haven't had success with reading for fun. When you *read,* anything that doesn't attract you can go straight back on the shelf. As we talked about before, most assigned works will naturally fall under *ugh* reading simply because you're required to read them. But it may also have to do with the content—especially if you've given your English class your best shot, approached each new novel with utmost effort, and still found them deathly boring. Don't give up on reading. You just haven't been exposed to fun reading yet. I'll talk about this more in "Genre Shifting," but just like with any other medium, you've got to pick and choose what to read based on what will engage you. It's just like scrolling through content on Netflix. If you know you're a *Parasite* fan, are you sure you'll enjoy *Tall Girl 2*?

Remember the *Rainbow Magic* fairies from childhood? What about the *Magic Treehouse* books? *Junie B. Jones*? *Geronimo Stilton*? Surely, you've not forgotten *Diary of a Wimpy Kid*. What made these books so appealing? Certainly, we wouldn't enjoy reading them nearly as much now as we did back then (except *Diary of a Wimpy Kid;* that series is timeless). When we were children, we fell directly into these series' target audience. The books were quite literally made for us. These authors knew what our age group enjoyed and would consume, and they wrote those elements into their work.

When you read any book, you become a member of that book's audience. As a reader, you get to choose what you read. You'll have greater luck when you select a book that has been tailored for you, written with a group like you at the forefront of the author's mind. Identify which group you fall into—factor in age, preferred genre, content level…anything else that will help you feel more at home with a text. By doing this, you're actively separating *ugh* reading from your fun reading and setting yourself up for success.

A DIFFERENT KIND OF READING

So now we know why so many people find it difficult to reach for a book by choice. The good news is that *ugh* literature makes up a very, very small portion of all that's available out there for you to read, even if it's all that you've been exposed to thus far. A characteristic unique to good literature, as opposed to other entertainment, is that it shouldn't feel like entertainment—yet it does. As we've discussed before, reading is often associated with being a "nerd," and nerds, stereotypically, don't know how to have fun. Therefore, books must not be fun, right? Take that entire connotation and throw it out.

Have you ever considered why so many movies have been created from books? It's almost like the automatic reaction to a popular book is a movie adaptation of it. Literature is perceived as a less digestible medium for the masses than film, which is why written stories are often modified for theaters. But too frequently during that conversion a lot of important content, narrative, and emotion is lost. Very, very often, the book is inherently better than the movie. Keep that in mind as you consider reading for leisure.

•••

The physical visual of a book exudes this connotation of old knowledge, almost as if all of them are guaranteed to contain extravagant wisdom. Dramas and films and even books themselves will depict towering columns of leather-bound volumes, draping them in a veil of untouchability. Surely, in some movie or show or game over the years, you've come across a secret, treasured library of precious tomes. In all probability, it was housed in a sprawling, stone mansion or an underground chamber lit with warm, yellow light. Blowing a thick layer of dust off some all-knowing Bible-thick book as eerie, hopeful music plays is also not an uncommon scene in the media. As easy as it is to get drawn to the implication that books are mysterious keepers of deep knowledge, it's just as easy to take that representation and assume that books are not for you.

Surely a novel that looks super long will be super boring. If it's old it'll be out of touch, the language will be complicated, and you won't like it, right? Wrong. Don't be intimidated by reading—that's like being afraid of a piece of paper. A book in its entirety might

HOW TO READ FOR FUN

seem enormously daunting at first (fair, some books can be several inches thick), but reading it won't be any different than reading a collection of pamphlets as thin as your nail. In fact, you'll quickly learn that a certain length of book is often required to achieve a certain level of quality. This isn't necessarily true for every kind of book, but for fiction especially? No immersive, detailed story is easily created in under a few hundred pages. *Harry Potter and the Prisoner of Azkaban* is 317 pages. *The Hunger Games* is 374 pages. *Divergent* is 487 pages. *The Hate U Give* is 444 pages. You get the idea.

It's also very important to acknowledge that reading isn't a single-faceted thing. Imagine anything, anything at all, and someone's likely written a book about it. In fact, "reading" isn't constrained to novel-type compositions either. There are magazines, articles, fanfiction… technically even the news counts. Reading for fun does not mean you need to sit straight-backed at your homework desk with a copy of *The Grapes of Wrath*. If Steinbeck's depiction of the Great Depression is your comfort story, go right ahead. But you can also read about the secrets of manipulation (*The 48 Laws of Power*), tales of glittering fairy adventures (*Rainbow Magic*), or the loopholes to monetary success (*Rich Dad, Poor Dad*), if that better interests you.

The beauty of writing is that it can encapsulate anything from philosophical musings to petty, social gossip. All the benefits of reading that we talked about in chapter one? The even greater beauty is that they'll come to you no matter what you choose to read. Granted, a research article will gift you different knowledge than a romance novel, but a universal constant of literature is learning. No matter what you read or how well the author has written, there is always a lesson to be learned.

The literature you've come across thus far does not at all define the stories that are waiting for you to pick them up. Reading isn't work, and reading isn't a chore. Once you're able to make the distinction between *ugh* reading and *reading*, you're well on your way to enjoying literature for fun.

CHAPTER 3

The Approach

AS WITH ANY NEW HOBBY, THE WAY YOU approach learning to read for fun is critical to your success. So far, it's been difficult to perceive reading as something that should be done by choice, much less enjoyed. Now it's time to move past what's been going wrong and start learning how to do it better.

In this chapter I'll talk about how to focus, both before you read and during. Then we'll discuss endurance: its importance, strategies, and applications—particularly regarding classic novels. With the right approach, making the choice to read can become easy. Far easier than a lot of people make it for themselves, and much more fun than you might expect.

HOW TO FOCUS

Focus: the eternal struggle. It's a hard battle that few of us ever learn to control, and even fewer learn to fully conquer. Once you have a mind to do something, your ability to actually get it done depends on your capability to concentrate on the task at hand. It's ridiculously easy to allow your thoughts to drift elsewhere simply because there's too much to think about.

This is especially relevant in terms of reading, something that can easily be as boring as it can be fun. You might be in the middle of a page, suddenly remember you're going to a dinner party that night, and start mentally planning your outfit. An unbidden embarrassing memory from seventh grade might crop up. Or maybe a friend just broke up with their boyfriend and you're thinking up ways for them to respond. In all these cases, there's no way the page in front of you is going to be able to hold your full attention for long. Being able to shut out intrusive thoughts is your key to giving each book a fair chance. Focusing on the words in front of you will be critical to understanding its story, picking up key details, and being able to absorb the book as it was intended to be read. If your attention is inconsistent, it'll be too easy to mistake a good novel for a bad one.

The importance of focus starts from the moment you decide to read to the moment you close the cover. As important as it is to endure *while* you read, the battle begins before you even turn the first page.

Meet Bryan. Bryan has a book in hand. He's cleared out his schedule for the next half hour, he's mustered conviction and courage, and he is truly ready to read. Just as he's about to snuggle into the couch and crack the cover, though, his throat itches. Naturally, he speed-walks down to the kitchen for a quick glass of water before he begins, because he really did want to finally get to that book today. As the glass fills, Bryan catches a glimpse of the news channel his dad has had on the television at unnecessarily high volume for the past hour or so. There's an interesting story being reported: some guy's leading the police on a car chase down a highway not far from his cousins' place. Soon Bryan's standing in his living room in his fuzzy slippers, chatting about the man's impressive escape, book all but forgotten. Out of the corner of his eye Bryan accidentally catches a glimpse of the clock—suddenly his reading time is halfway gone.

Bryan had the motivation to read; he was fully prepared to settle down and give it his best. But his real obstacle was actually getting to the task itself. Being able to put yourself into the right mindset to read requires effort, but opening the cover and reading each page thoroughly requires consistent concentration. You can always quit reading a book if it's *that* bad, but only after you've given it a chance. To make sure you're giving a novel your best attempt, I'll take you through three steps that have helped me focus before and during reading. (I know giving you a step-by step procedure is awfully '*ugh* reading' of me, but bear with me—it'll help.)

1. DESIGNATE
First up is to designate. Designate a time and a place. To be able to focus on your reading, other distractions and interference with activities throughout your day must be minimized. Sitting down and beginning to read might be easy for you, but if your mind wanders every two minutes to the latest project you were work-

ing on or the job application you're waiting to hear back from, you won't be able to truly engage with the book. When and where you read throughout your day don't always have to be the same, but actively planning ahead and designating a time and place will make sure you actually begin the reading (especially in the beginning). When the designated time comes around, or you look at the place where you're supposed to read (say, your couch), it'll remind you that you have to get started soon.

2. ISOLATE

Next up is isolation. I mean this in every sense of the word. As you gear up to read, physically isolate yourself from others, distance yourself from anything that will distract you from reading, turn off your phone and toss it to the other side of the room. *But what if it's on vibrate only? Do not disturb? It's completely off but I just want to keep it next to me!* Nope. Simply having it by your side will trigger the reflex to check for notifications every once in a while, and each glimpse you get of it is a reminder of the world you're supposed to be leaving behind for a little while. Make sure your phone (or any similar distractor) is either across the room or far enough away that you won't be tempted to reach for it. The majority of focusing effectively comes from your ability to separate the task at hand and the rest of your undoubtedly busy life—and physically doing so makes all the difference. If you have siblings or parents, make sure they won't be barging in and starting conversations as you try to read. Of course, be kind about it, but especially in the beginning, reading is a solitary sport. And remember, isolation should happen not only visually but audibly as well. It's important to find a relatively quiet location—if there is an unavoidable amount of noise, it's best to find an area where it all blends together. Maybe even consider earplugs or noise-cancelling headphones if those would work better for you. As peculiar as it may seem at first to sit alone in a silent room with all entertaining possessions tossed to the side, it will pay off when you discover how much simpler it becomes to engage with the story.

3. GLUE

Finally, as silly as it sounds, teach yourself to glue. Glue your eyes to the page, glue your body to your seat, glue your hands to the book. It's all too easy to put a story down for a "one minute break," get up and walk around, and abandon it for the rest of the night (like Bryan). For as long as you've designated your time for reading, let's say fifteen minutes, you should try your very best to stay in the same spot, in relatively the same position. If you know you'll be needing a break as your reading periods get longer, think ahead and designate some time for those in your reading plan. And be sure to prepare beforehand! Bryan's quest to go find water ended up costing him a lot of his designated time, so be sure to collect everything you'll need and keep it by you.

...

This sounds like a lot, I know. But the good news is that you won't have to deliberately take these steps more than a few times. While building a habit, which is, in our case, reading for fun, it shouldn't take too much additional effort to continue good practices as long as you start off strong. The faster you train yourself to focus while reading, the easier it will come to you and the longer you'll be able to read without extra effort. You won't need to consider three defined steps to achieve concentration—you'll likely begin to designate, isolate, and glue by subconscious habit whenever you settle down to read. So, although it may feel a bit cumbersome now, implementing good focus habits from the very beginning will prevent you from having to learn away distracted reading practices later.

ENDURANCE

So now we know how to focus. When reading for fun, let's assume you're implementing all the best practices: you won't be distracted, you'll want to read, and your area will be essentially distraction-free. And yet there's still a chance that you'll find reading difficult. In an ideal world, every book would be easy to start and easy to get through with the right attitude, but in reality that often isn't the case. There will be times when you simply start to disengage with a book, even if you had been going along and enjoying the story just fine minutes before. This happens to everyone, and it can happen for a few different reasons.

One could be that you've drained the amount of motivation you had for reading. Check your purpose. Are you enjoying yourself? Do you remember why you started reading for fun in the first place? If what you're reading is no longer enjoyable to you, set the book down and take a break. This is so important—pushing on when you genuinely don't want to is the fastest way to develop resentment towards something. However, if you know you want to keep going, make sure you remind yourself of *why* before you do. Adopting the correct mindset, and resetting it when it strays, is critical to being able to enjoy your reading and continue with it.

Take Jo March, the lovable protagonist of Little Women (the 2019 movie's plot). She's obsessed, and I mean obsessed, with writing. It's her passion; it's her thing. Jo March is to writing as Beyoncé is to music. Yet we see throughout the course of her story that she is only able to write successfully and enjoy writing when she's in the right headspace. Jo begins her writing by penning stories for fun, for her family, and for herself. When she initially reaches out with her compositions, she's able to publish in papers and win awards—and at first these only serve to assure her of her talent. Later in life, though, she moves to New York for a career. Here, the purpose of her writing gradually shifts away from passion to approval, publication, and ultimately compensation. She writes only what she thinks her publisher wants to see and becomes angry when her work isn't taken. When one of her best friends in New York critiques her writing, she lashes out at him—we can watch the way she falls out of love with writing—and eventually Jo ends up literally burning several of her stories.

When Jo's little sister, Beth, becomes frighteningly ill, Jo drops everything to return home. Immersed once again in the environment where she learned to love writing for itself, she's reminded of what it meant to her. When a dejected Jo tells her sister that she cannot write anymore, Beth tells her to write a story for her and reminds her why she does what she does: "You are a writer. Before anyone knew or paid you."

Eventually Jo regains her fire and her connection with writing by remembering this moment, but we can take away from it, too. Jo finds writing simple and enjoyable when she's in the right mindset and working towards the right purpose. Be sure to reflect this in your reading. Chores are supposed to get done no matter how tired or unmotivated or unhappy you are, but remember that reading should never be a chore. Wait until you've reached an optimistic, or at least determined, mindset to attempt your reading. A negative attitude will get you nowhere, and it'll drive you away from whatever you're trying to read. And like Jo, we all need to remember sometimes why we do what we do. Don't forget the reason you started your literary journey, or even this book. Why do you read? If you find that the answers have become all the wrong reasons, put the book down and reset.

But apart from mindset or rationale, any struggle you experience with endurance might simply be because you have been reading for too long. As a very general rule, humans are only able to concentrate on one thing for about 45 minutes, which means that if you've been at something for over an hour you should expect to find yourself slowing down. Being eager and ambitious is fantastic, but don't go overkill and fry your eyes by reading for hours on end. Pace yourself and read what you can. Although having endurance is important, don't get frustrated if you find yourself disengaging when you've already been at it for a while. And for some, especially in the beginning, keep in mind that your endurance threshold might begin extremely low. Maybe fifteen minutes is all you can possibly make yourself do on the first day you read for leisure. But as with most things reading, the more you practice the easier it will become. As the plot thickens and your stamina builds, you'll find yourself lost in the pages for longer and longer.

The sudden inability to engage with a book could also simply be because the book itself has hit a lull. There is always a point when there's nothing more you can do as a reader to make a book more engaging than it is. If you find yourself simply unable to connect with a novel, don't be afraid to set it down and try another time. Or try a different book entirely. Like we've talked about before, this journey is all about you, and that means that you can quite literally read whatever you want. Why waste precious time on boring literature? That being said, don't take giving up on books lightly. Many pieces start out slow but build into masterpieces—it's just a side effect of the nature of written stories. In order to build a plot, it must be introduced in the beginning of the book. The more complex an author's world is, the more context they'll have to provide, and unfortunately these parts of novels can often feel stagnant. I'd say that as a rule of thumb you should try to get at least a third through any given book before letting go, but that's not to say you shouldn't trust your gut if you just *know* you won't like a book.

And lastly, there is this phenomenon that's dubbed "book hangover." It's also sometimes called "book withdrawal," and what the term essentially means is that you're unable to move onto another book because the one you've just finished was too good. It may seem utterly ridiculous now, but book hangovers do exist. This is the feeling you'll get after your first soul-altering book. You read a masterpiece—a heart-wrenching, mind-bending novel, and suddenly it's over. Done. The characters, the story, the world you've just spent the last few hours getting attached to? Gone. Now it's hard to read any other book because it feels like nothing will ever compare.

During a book hangover, you might be afraid to start reading again because you feel there's absolutely no way that what you encounter next will be nearly as good as what you've just read; you don't even want to try. This happens with movies and other art as well—anything that is able to alter perception so effectively is difficult to forget, and it's our nature to compare everything thereafter to the perfection of that work. If this happens, consider it a good thing! It means you've achieved a level of bookworm that is hard to accomplish. It is difficult, however, to recover, and moving on often requires just as much endurance as actually getting through a book. Keep in mind that no matter how good what you've just read might have been, there is always more out there.

...

On the off chance that none of these apply, let's say you simply find yourself unable to keep reading for as long as you want to. How to build your literary endurance? First, ensure you've followed through on all the steps to effective focus. Remember to designate, isolate, and glue, because the easiest way to break endurance is by distraction. Secondly, try to engage in the plot by following a particular character throughout the course of the book. This is particularly effective if you're reading a book that's been written from multiple perspectives—the multitude of storylines can quickly become confusing, and the spacing between each part of the same perspective can make it difficult to engage. In a single point-of-view works, this strategy can help you center on the plotline rather than getting caught up in atmospheric details. But regardless of the format of the literature, always, *always*, remember your purpose. Despite how grim this might sound, sometimes some grit and motivation are really all you need to

READING THE CLASSICS

Since we're on the topic of endurance, we may as well touch on the ultimate test of perseverance: the classics. Reading a classic novel has the potential to be either the best experience of your life or the worst. It's a whole different world of literature, because these books were often written in a different time, context, and dialect than ours. If reading was a sport, this would be like the final meet of the season or the last stretch of the track—the most difficult but potentially most rewarding. And as we all know: where there's no risk, there's no reward.

Personally, I struggle with classic books quite a bit. It took me all summer to get through *The Grapes of Wrath* (which has won a Pulitzer Prize and the National Book Award), but I still found it unfulfilling. No matter how much I read, how focused I was, and how much determination I had, it simply wasn't the right fit for me. Remember that you might be doing everything right and the book just may not be for you. This applies to any reading you approach, but keep it in mind with classics especially. Do give it your best shot, but understand that this literature wasn't written to go down smooth.

The first classic that I was truly able to enjoy was *Pride and Prejudice* by Jane Austen. Go figure—it's a romance. What really struck me was that although the language is definitely not the modern English we're used to, the emotion rang true. A story of finery, societal maneuvering, wit, romance, and family, all with a touch of enemies-to-lovers? Perfection. Not to mention the fantastic movie adaptation available once I had finished the book (The 2005 *Pride and Prejudice* is by far a favorite).

Classic literature offers you a glimpse into a different time, and because of this, it is extremely effective in expanding both vocabulary and comprehension skills. If you're looking for something that'll give you a heavy dose of language-arts related aptitude, this might be a genre you find yourself interested in. This quality of classics is also why a lot of students grew up despising them—English classes often go very, very heavy on classic literature. But with the right approach you might find such books a worthy endeavor.

If you're really into the weightiness of classics but find yourself unable to comprehend them, most also have abridged versions. They offer the same story in a more familiar jargon, and while they may not carry the exact same significance, well done abridged editions can offer the same skillful plot and induce similar emotion as the original. Classic literature is certainly not easy, but it'll put your endurance to the test like no other. If you get curious one day, don't shy away from well-known or old titles—they may hold stories you'll treasure for the rest of your life.

CONSISTENCY IS NOT ALWAYS KEY

The last step to approach is consistency. Being as consistent as possible with your reading is key to solidifying it as an enjoyable habit. But to be honest—despite how much I might preach "Reading is good for you! Do it as often as you can!"—I've gone stretches of nearly a month without sitting down and reading a book just for myself. It's way too easy to start treating work as your "daily reading quota." That essay you just submitted? The chapter of *To Kill a Mockingbird* due tomorrow? Those terms and conditions you just read through? As much as we might want them to, sorry, they don't count.

Sometimes you're able to read, but just don't want to. I'd know—it happens to me all the time. Maybe you're in the middle of a particularly drab book, or you're just about to start a new reading that hasn't captured your heart yet. Sometimes you're really just not in the mood. And that's okay. The biggest key to reading for fun is just that: it's for fun.

Reading for fun means that you'll never be forced to read any particular amount at any particular speed, and you can always control what you read. It's incredibly important to read things that genuinely interest you, especially at the beginning of your reading journey. And don't forget, it's all about you. That means you *can* give up on a book if it's absolutely horrid. You can re-read your favorite books (even out of series order!). And if you really, truly can't bring yourself to do it, no one's forcing you to read at all.

Some days you'll pick up a book and set it down without turning a single page. Some days you'll try not to even glance at it at all. Reading is an individual, customizable journey, and the blessing in that is that everything is completely up to you. Readers read simply because we want to. It's alright to take a day or a few off. Sometimes forcing yourself to do something is counter-productive, because it trains your mind to think of it as another task to check off your list instead of something that is genuinely beneficial.

That's the key difference between the kind of reading you'll now be doing and the reading that you have been forced to do. With work, assignments, and text-

HOW TO READ FOR FUN

book readings (in other words, *ugh* reading), there's always the feeling of *have to*. You *have to* finish this chapter. You *have to* read this by Wednesday. You *have to* think on the significance of the green light at the end of the dock and find it profound. When you read for fun, you take away that *have to*. Anything enjoyable should inherently be optional—if someone forces you to do something you wanted to do anyways, it takes away half the fun. You're able to choose the when, what, and where of your reading. So whenever you do, keep this in mind. There's no *have to*, and you're not back in the classroom. You're doing this for you, and no one else.

CHAPTER 4

Making Time

MAKING TIME IS HARD. IT'S HARD ESPECIALLY with so many other things on your plate, so many deadlines and expectations and too-short nights. And it's even harder when you're trying to make time for something new. Reading in particular is something that's completely different for everyone, so you likely don't know exactly what literature you'll enjoy yet or what you'll have to do to get there. Maybe you aren't sure it's worth it to read every day in proportion to how long it might take. Maybe you aren't sure if the effort making room in your schedule will take is worth it. There's just never *time*.

Finding time is understandably the most common struggle I've heard thus far. It's single-handedly been the largest roadblock for most prospective readers, including myself. Time is our scarcest resource, so if you're struggling to piece together enough for school, work, and self-care, who's got the space to add reading to that already overflowing plate?

Reading for fun is something that truly depends on how much you *want* to do it. If you're passionate, curious, or determined enough, the urge to read will come inherently with time. Until then, all it takes is the right approach. In this chapter, we'll talk about how to make time to read while allowing that natural urge to grow.

PRIORITY

Making time, for anything, requires you to reorder your priorities. The great thing about reading for fun is that once you find the first book you genuinely enjoy, it'll naturally make you want to read other things like it. This kicks off the chain reaction of wanting to pick up a book in your free time, staying put a few extra minutes just to finish off a chapter, or maybe even pondering over a storyline while you go about your day. Once you reach this phase, you've successfully learned to read for fun.

Right now, though, it's likely that reading isn't very high on your list of daily priorities. Hopefully, by the time you do get around to finishing your first book it will have shifted up a few slots. The goal is to let reading grow in your favor as it becomes less of a chore and more like a kind of break to you. This is a natural process, and it's the same process that separates book lovers from those who cringe at the sight of a novel. You'll be hard-pressed to find anyone, even among those who proudly call themselves bookworms, who reads every single day without fail. But the reason why they're able to keep going back to it is because reading rests fairly high on their list. If you love something, even if you can't get to it every day, it's something you will choose to do whenever you can. This habit of consistency is what we're ultimately trying to obtain—you want to find yourself willing to reach for a book whenever you find a free moment.

Every reader has learned their love for reading through a process. No one wakes up one day to suddenly find themselves an accomplished reader with the constant urge to read for years and years and years. No one is born with the ability to read, which means that becoming a reader is a skill that is taught. And you can teach yourself. There are always days when a lack of time prevents even a glance at a novel. We're all on the same journey of fitting literature into our lives, and like nearly everything on this journey, making time will get much easier the more you practice it. But to begin, you'll need to make reading a priority.

What is a priority? What does making reading a priority even entail? A priority is something that you regard as more important than many other things you do. It takes precedence over other alternatives for how you spend your time. What priority *doesn't* mean, though, is adding anything stressful to your plate. Remember, this is a journey you chose for yourself—you should not be sacrificing anything major for reading. It's a *pastime*, not work. For example, prioritizing reading over watching Netflix might mean that you'd postpone watching your next episode of *The Vampire Diaries* and read the final chapter of *The Notebook* instead. We're naturally predisposed to consider our personal priorities worth 'more', and therefore we are willing to give them more effort and time. If reading for fun is something you truly want to get into, adding it to your list of priorities might just have you finding time for it—time you might not have even known you had.

Like any new hobby, reading for fun will have to start relatively high on your agenda. It's likely near the very bottom right now, but try to push it up and keep it up there for as long as you can. As consuming literature becomes less strenuous and more like a habit for you, it will move down to settle somewhere wherever it fits best on your list of priorities. This is what makes the beginning so hard.

How can you just push reading that high on your list? It might help to reconsider all the benefits reading can give you. Consider it an investment—a small sacrifice for a large, long-term return. Next, think about *when* you're choosing to read. By reading at that moment, what are you giving up? Is it the next episode of *Gilmore Girls*? Extra homework? Sleep? Weigh those costs and benefits, and if the other activity is worth more to you, change when you read. If we're to utilize reading as a relaxant, it won't do to have it interrupt the other important parts of your life. Instead, make sure the changes you make to your weekly routine are both positive and feasible.

The key to being able to prioritize reading without developing a bitterness toward it is the minimization of the disruption it causes to the other parts of your life. Making reading a priority doesn't mean you should start a new chapter when you've got a 20-page journal article due the next day. It means knowing when you *can* read and being sure to follow through. It also means remembering that you always have an out. You don't have to force yourself to want to open, or even touch, a book just yet. If you couldn't bear to complete those seventeen assigned pages for class last week, it obviously wouldn't make sense to expect yourself to be ready to leap into written worlds. Prioritizing reading, in this context, just means that you get to it as often as *possible*. If that means reading one paragraph a day in the beginning, that's how it'll be. Never forget that reading for fun is a choice, and a choice that is always worth it if you approach it right. Making reading a priority is the first step to making time for it.

STRATEGY

Once you get the ball rolling, opening a book has the potential to become as comfortable a motion as checking your phone in the morning. In theory, we'd love to read a chapter every morning, with lunch, and before bed. If reading came as easily as watching Netflix, we'd likely spend hours on it daily, no problem. A really good book will eventually be able to make you feel this way, if everything ends up going perfectly. But right now it isn't that easy. So how to make time for it? What if reading for fun was required, like math homework? It might be easier to motivate yourself to get to it each day if it was written on your to-do list.

Although a large part of our goal here is to distinguish reading from the frustration of a chore, treating it like a box to be checked off might be a necessary step to getting started. The central difference is in the fact that reading will quickly (hopefully) become something you enjoy, while chores will likely forever remain dull.

Try setting deadlines for yourself, at least for the first few chapters of your chosen title. Think in terms of blocks of words, not in pages, because it's much harder to restart your reading in the middle of a page than at the beginning of a chapter. Think of how much easier it is to follow along if you watch a new show from episode to episode as compared to resuming it halfway through a scene. Similarly, read text the way it was meant to be read—in chapters or sections. If even these require a determination that you cannot muster at the moment, you can also read to the shorter scene breaks (in this book they're indicated by three dots in-between paragraphs). These are developed pauses within the writing, which means that when you start again it will be easier to re-engage and less likely that you'll need to go back and read for context.

Physically writing down your reading plan can also help with making time. Looking at those deadlines will help you keep a healthy pressure on yourself to not give up before you've even started, and completing them can make you feel satisfied as well as productive. Doing this will help you make reading "required," at least in the very beginning. A deadline provides an obligation to yourself that offers a reward when accomplished, and at the same time it gives you a set timeline that'll help you split an overwhelmingly large book into small, attainable sections. Although treating your reading as a requirement arguably isn't inherently fun, it'll get you started with a book. The book itself, if it's right for you, will do the rest of the convincing.

To keep each experience positive, make sure you're being realistic when you set your deadlines. Remember, reading for fun is all about what *you* want. As often as possible is best, but if you simply don't have the space in your schedule to read every day? Don't make that part of your deadline. Plan realistically and plan kindly—don't set yourself up with crazy expectations that you know you're bound to struggle with.

•••

A big part of why we define our goals and write them down is to hold ourselves accountable. If that is difficult for you (it is for me), don't worry. What are friends for? There are plenty of ways to drag your friends, relatives, or even strangers into your reading journey to encourage accountability. Share book lists with your friends. Trade recommendations with your family. Sit down and actually read with one another. This is bound to make your book-crazy friend ecstatic.

You? Reading? Finally! Reading with someone else, simultaneously, is a fantastic way to hold both of you to each others' expectations while sharing a great experience together. Books are fantastic ways to start conversation and learn more about your friend (and learn about their red flags—team Peeta or Gale?).

It's essentially peer pressure at its finest. If your book buddy has already read this week's chapter, you can't let them down by skimping on your reading, can you? Plus, it can be so fun to debate theories and discuss characters with another person. You're jumping into a new world together. This can also keep you motivated through lulls of the text—nothing's stopping you from complaining about a book to each other as well.

And if you don't have a willing friend, join a book club! Find someone online. Be safe, but there are thousands of people, millions actually, who are looking to read with someone else online. Goodreads, Fable, and discussion platforms like Quora and Reddit are all filled with people ready to jump into the pages with you. They might even have a set reading plan already (or a flexible one), if that's what you want. If you're looking to share the wealth yourself, you can also volunteer at your local library—most are often looking for readers to share books with children and help introduce literature to the young community.

It's not for everyone, but reading with someone else can make it twice the fun. Consider using a buddy as a tool to hold yourself accountable while getting the most out of what you read.

SITUATION

Reading shouldn't be a burden as long as you don't allow yourself to feel that way. Start small, and eventually you'll want to spend longer and longer with your nose in a book. Once you're invested in a story, it'll feel easier to keep reading rather than putting the book down. You're going to *want*, sometimes even *need*, to know how it all ends. But how do we get to that point? All you have to do is structure each day to involve some amount of reading. When we talked about our approach, we talked about designation. As we worked on prioritizing, we created goals to help you introduce consistent reading practices to your schedule. Now we'll work on implementing such practices in each day.

I went to a small, suburban elementary school, where, in general, the kids were lucky enough to have parents who'd worked hard to ensure that their childrens' only worries were which Lunchable they'd get for the day or who they'd play with at recess. The other seven-year-olds and I spent our time playing ball, catching ladybugs, and drawing massive lines of hopscotch. Oddly enough, a lot of my peers at the time also enjoyed reading. They'd read at lunch next to the kids squirting their GoGurt tubes at the ceiling; during class (enough that our teacher would have to tell the class to pay attention and read later during free time); and even during recess, tucked away underneath trees and in the playground slides as the literature swallowed them whole.

In second grade, my class had a daily "reading hour." At the beginning of each month, we'd all march single file down to the school library, where each of us would select a book. Every day during that month, we were then given about half an hour to immerse ourselves in the stories we'd chosen. Granted, some kids never did get to finishing that first chapter, and there were days when I would "discreetly" fold origami cootie catchers behind my propped open book, but that half-hour was a unanimously enjoyed time for my fellow seven-year-olds and me.

If you think about it, kids are far more likely to read for fun than their adult counterparts. Is it because they have more time? Maybe. But they also have attention spans miles shorter than their elders. So why do so many more children express a love for reading than adults? Part of it might be the lack of "more important" things to do, or the magnetism a good story has to an imaginative young mind. But many kids grew up being told that reading is a good thing, that they should read, and that they *had* to read in school. A lot of us can surely remember being forced to sit and read for a while at least a few times a week, either in school or at home. Once you grow up, no one can really tell you to do that anymore. I mean, it's not like your boss will tell you to "go home and read for fun for at least thirty minutes tonight."

The kind of structure that kids had who were taught to enjoy reading is the same kind we should attempt to create for ourselves. You'll need to create the framework, but it will feel much more instinctive to enjoy literature after that. Children who were encouraged to foster a love for reading were often given times where they had nothing better to do, like my class's reading hour. During that hour reading was the only option. Try to find moments to read when it is the *best* option.

For many, the best times to read are when you are physically comfortable. This lets you engage with the book while resting your mind and body, so it can easily serve as a gentle start or a calming wind-down to a day. If it helps, the time you set apart for reading doesn't have to be a part of your day at all. You can think of it as a sort of pre-sleep ritual. Plus, keeping a book on your nightstand will encourage you to open it nearly every night (or morning). Consider setting up each day for success using just ten minutes before bed every night—such small changes can have much larger repercussions than they appear to have. (Be sure to stay aware of time if you choose to do this, though! There's always the danger of getting *too* comfortable, and before you know it you could be nose-deep in a mystery novel at two in the morning .)

You can also use some of the quiet moments throughout your daily, or weekly, routine to get a little page-turning in. Do you have a few minutes after you get home from work? What about transportation—could you read while riding the train, bus, or while someone else is driving? Planes are an excellent place to read, by the way. Or what about that peaceful time you get on Saturday mornings, when the rest of the house is still asleep? The pause between your breakfast and your workout, the gap after dinner and before homework, the hour you spend on TikTok right after school? What if you tried reading during those increments? Set aside some extra time throughout your week to just sit, relax, and read for a bit. They don't have to be long chunks of time.

This is *your* journey, and you get to work on it whenever it best fits you. Setting aside a predetermined period for you to focus only on reading will make it far easier for you to get engaged, stay consistent, and meet your goals. This applies to nearly any new skill or hobby you try to adopt—before you fall in love with something, you've got to give it a chance, right? Well, the time you find for reading is you giving it that chance. Once you're able to give reading the amount of time it needs, you're well on your way to doing it for fun.

CHAPTER 5

Finding Good Books

SO YOU'RE READY TO READ, BUT WHERE TO start? Once you're committed to reading, there's a few steps you'll need to take to ensure that reading will be *fun*. I won't lie, some authors are just people who like to hear themselves talk for ages on paper—but some can transport you out of this world into theirs. That's why it's so important to select the right content. There are millions of books out there, and it's important that you start somewhere that'll be enjoyable to you. So how to sort through so many options? How to find the books you want? In this chapter we'll talk about what to read and where to find it.

GENRE SIFTING

The most important thing about your journey to becoming a reader might just be what books you're reading. Obviously, if you're an adventure fan who's only reading self-help books, you won't enjoy yourself nearly as much as you could. Likewise, if you're reading to get tangible information out of books, while stories do teach lessons, fantasy novels might not be your most productive choice.

Think of it in terms of choosing a sport to play. Let's say you know you want to start learning a new sport, but you have no idea where to begin. If you've got a lithe, petite figure and enjoy dancing, it's likely you'd be much better suited for gymnastics than wrestling. In fact, if you chose to begin your athletic journey in such an ill-suited sport, it's very possible you'd find yourself disinterested, get injured, or end up otherwise unsuccessful. The fumbled experience might even warn you away from trying other sports. But what if you'd chosen gymnastics instead? It incorporates elements you already enjoy and fits your structure well. You'd have a far easier time and much more fun. You might even be encouraged to go on to try other sports, like figure skating or diving.

It's the same way with literature. You're beginning with little to no experience in reading for fun, and we don't want to leave a bad taste on your tongue with a rough first start. Spending a bit of time discovering different forms and genres will start your relationship with reading off on the right foot. This is what I like to call "genre sifting." Expose yourself to lots of different types of literature, keeping in mind what you want to gain out of reading, or what sounds fun to you. As you do so, cross genres that don't interest you off the list as you see fit. In other words, sift through genres until you're left with only the ones you're excited about. Once you're down to your final pickings, finding a popular book from that category is always a safe move.

There's much more out there than your typical fiction story. Even just at your local library, you'll find spiritual, historical, astrological, self-identity, and biographical titles on top of the expected fantasy, realistic fiction, sci-fi, and mystery. There's also a large range of self-improvement literature, including how-to books like this one. You'll find drama, romance, poetry, comedy, mythology, essay collections, survival stories… anything you want to read about is waiting for you. Take this opportunity to find something that will really interest you—it's your journey, after all.

I'd recommend avoiding any very niche subjects in the beginning. Reading a very specified work will reduce your ability to branch out from it later, because you've started with literature whose characteristics are unlikely to be replicated in other writings. This decreases the size of your potential reading material and can make it scarier to try new genres. At least in the beginning, think big. Once you've established a type of book that you know you enjoy and can fall back on, you can always branch out.

Want somewhere to start? Here's a list of the most expansive genres that you may encounter at a library or bookstore. Keep in mind that this list is not all-inclusive, and that each one has many subgenres that are likely to interest you as well!

FICTION
- CLASSICS

- FANTASY
- SCIENCE FICTION
- GRAPHIC NOVELS
- MYSTERY
- POETRY
- ROMANCE
- ADVENTURE
- DYSTOPIA
- HORROR

NONFICTION

- MEMOIR
- BIOGRAPHY
- INFORMATIONAL
- SELF-HELP
- ESSAYS

The fact that you've chosen to read opens up incredible opportunities. You can read absolutely whatever you want! Within each category there is a staggering amount of literature that you can choose from, and fantastic books lie in every genre.

PICKING A BOOK: THE LIBRARY

Once you know what *kind* of book you want to read, how do you even begin to pick one? I wouldn't recommend randomly selecting a good-looking book off a library shelf for two reasons. First, this reduces your chance of reading something you'll genuinely enjoy on the first try. This goes back to that bitter taste we were talking about—it's best to begin with something that you know you'll have the highest chances of really having fun with. (That's not to say that researching the title beforehand will guarantee that you enjoy the book, but at least this way you're increasing your probability of liking the story.)

Second, by selecting a random book off a shelf, you'd quite literally be judging the book by its cover. While it's true that the quality of some, *some,* books can be determined by their cover, the packaging of a book is often a much better reflection of its publisher's standards than the book's contents. Most authors don't even get a say in their cover design, so you're better off withholding that judgment for the pages inside. Also, if you're at a bookstore or library, remember that well-worn covers don't necessarily mean they're old any more than they mean that the stories they hold are loved. Some of the best books I've read have been housed under fusty, unaesthetic, flimsy covers. So just remember, looks can be deceiving.

But how to judge beyond a book's looks? On every book, there will be a quick blurb about the main plotline on either the inside cover (for hardcovers) or back cover (for paperbacks). These can give a pretty good summation of the ideas in a book, although they're also often manufactured by the publisher rather than the author. These descriptions are convenient, but they do also demonstrate the issue of "showing" vs "telling." Obviously, contracting thousands of words into a few sentences won't yield the same engagement the novel itself will. I've often read fantastic books that had a deceptively dull synopsis, so try to read between the lines. And if you just can't find any synopses that sound extremely engaging, I'd suggest taking a chance on the best book anyways. You never know.

•••

Once you've found the first book you want to try for fun, you'll likely want to check it out from a library. This way you'll be able to read without cost, and you won't have to commit to anything except returning the title in a few weeks' time. Don't forget that libraries allow you to renew books as well, so don't be put off by the time constraint! It's likely you'll have several weeks to read the book and often through renewal that time can stretch over months.

While it's not ideal to go pick a random library book as your very first introduction to reading for fun, a library run can be a very successful way to revamp your book list later on in your reading journey. Don't be overwhelmed by the rows and rows of novels. Instead, think of them as opportunities. Out of the thousands of books in the building, odds are that your new favorite is somewhere on a shelf inside. I'll help you make sense of the building and the books—I know it can be a lot.

If this is your first time in a particular library, it's a great idea to spend a minute or so surveying its layout and exploring. It's very possible they have options you wouldn't even guess they'd carry. For example, my local library has a floor-to-ceiling shelf of cookbooks and a section reserved specifically for books that preach positivity. It even has a small bookstore where you can buy donated books for $1 per hardcover (which is insanely low-priced!).

Once you've gotten your bearings, head to the section of the library that houses your chosen genre. There are different shelves, and sometimes different floors for various types of literature. You might want to check out multiple areas of the library, especially if you're trying to branch out. If you can't find a book you're looking for, it could just be in a different grouping, so make sure you've checked thoroughly! And don't be afraid to ask someone for help—librarians don't bite.

Many libraries divide their contents by age grouping, so also make sure you're not wandering around the children's section for a young adult (YA) fantasy. Age separations typically fall in the following categories: Children, Young Adult, New Adult, and Adult. The lines often blur for young adult and new adult novels. The main differences between these divisions are content and reading difficulty, although oftentimes categories overlap. Don't shy away from an adult book just because you're a teen or avoid a YA book just because you're an adult—many novels are placed in other age groups and sometimes authors even label their books as "adult" just to reach a wider audience.

Within those general regions of the library, there should be further divisions by genre. This will either be by shelf or bookcase, depending on how big your library or bookstore is. Whatever you're looking for, find the area where that kind of book is housed and head over.

Once you're in your chosen area, you can either browse covers or search by last name for the title you're looking for. There are also computers around the library that have catalogs—you can search by author, title, or keyword, and it'll tell you exactly where the book is or if it's been checked out. Nowadays there are often also movies, disks, or audiobook players the catalog will show that are available to borrow.

It all might sound a bit complicated now, but after your first few trips the process will feel deceptively simple. And while you're at the library, *please* remember to put books back in order after you've looked at them. This saves library staff and other readers a lot of headache.

To the order of discovering the right book, if you've got the time, it's always a nice idea to check online reviews before your visit. Reader reviews tend to be scathingly honest while giving you a better description of what the book really entails. If there's even a hint of romance in a novel, they'll be sure to let you know. It's also important to read reviews if you'd like trigger warnings. The mini blurbs on the covers won't explicitly detail any potential triggers, so it's up to you to avoid any accordingly. It's surprising how much

HOW TO READ FOR FUN

people are willing to write in reviews of literature; I've come across both scathing and gushing reviews that were the size of news articles.

A quick pre-library Google search might also help you create a quick list of books you want to search for while you're there. Especially on your first visit, this will be beneficial. It'll help you learn to navigate the library deliberately while alleviating the stress of walking in with no idea of what you're looking for, and if your first choice is checked out it will prevent you from walking out empty-handed. However, this can be a lot more effort than you're willing to commit to. Simply skimming the shelves of your chosen genre, reading an enticing-looking blurb, and taking the book home is completely okay too.

Before you commit to checking a book out, though, make sure to quickly flip through the pages. One time I was at my local library, and while browsing the YA section, I found a beautifully written inside-cover synopsis. I added the book to my stack and checked it out, excited to read the story. Upon getting home and opening the book, however, I was surprised with pages and pages of haikus rather than a continuous story. Do note that cover blurbs won't explicitly tell you the type of writing within, so it's always a good idea to quickly flip through. Not every book is a regular, typeset novel. You'll run across spine-bound interviews, text threads, poetry, and extremely unique writing styles that span hundreds of pages. If you're a Jeff Kinney fan, Virginia Woolfe might not sit the best with you. A few authors also choose to write in a very unique font, so if that type of thing bothers you, it's always useful to check. I'm not really one for poetry books, so I ended up deciding not to read the surprise book, and that's okay! I'll reiterate: this process is all about you, and the ultimate goal is to have fun. If you know you won't enjoy something, don't waste your time on it.

Also, don't be discouraged if your first experience isn't perfect. In fact, despite genre sifting, a perfect library run, or the employment of any other strategy, it's possible you just won't enjoy what you read. That's absolutely okay. Hopefully, every book you pick up will be worthwhile, but if the first couple aren't, don't give up. It's perfectly normal to have an unpleasant first experience in anything, but that doesn't reduce the value of what reading can do for you in the slightest. It's not you, it's the book, so keep sampling different works until you find something that catches your attention. Anyone can read for fun, including you, so although it's hard, don't give up on yourself before you've even started.

HARD COPY VS EBOOK

Now, we already know that reading is good for us. We've discussed strategies, goals, and advantages; we even know how to discern what to read—but for much of this book I've talked solely about novels. It's important not to forget that *any* literature, including articles, blogs, news forums…*any* such writing is fair game for the benefits reading can give you. Once you've chosen *what* you're going to read, you also get to choose the *how*. Hard copies are classic and well-loved, while eBooks and audiobooks are versatile and convenient. Both physical and virtual copies can be found for free, but there are a few distinguishing factors that can help you select your preference.

Reading by hard copy is my personal favorite. Evidence of over a thousand years' worth of history, the physical print of a favorite story simply can't be beat. It may sound bizarre to you now, but soon you might even begin to appreciate the smell of a book, or the velvety feel of its pages. Once you've read a couple books, their physical distinctions can start to become like characteristics, hints of the stories they hold inside. Crisp, white pages might mean a memoir, or perhaps its thin cover suggests concise yet inspiring remembrances inside. Softly tanned, ridged pages, however, are often characteristic of a grand adventure. They'll likely come with a thick hardcover, and house a saga of exciting tales. You'll also be able to see how far along you are in the story through the pages you've turned, which can help you measure your progress visually. These attributes all add up to your experience with a book, and it'll help you more deeply engage with its contents.

You've likely heard this before, but physical books also help give your eyes a break from screens. Don't we spend enough time on our computers and phones every day? The physical properties of a hard copy allow for entertainment and learning without a single blip of electricity, and this can help you enjoy yourself while disconnected. This might sound unfathomable right now, but eventually you might even find that there are moments when you prefer reading to texting, TikTok, or Netflix. This is a feeling that an eBook will not be able to give you nearly as effectively. Because you'll already be on a screen, it may be way easier for you to say "I'll finish this chapter after I respond to Anna's snapchat really quickly" or become otherwise distracted. It's also been studied that reading on paper yields higher comprehension than on a screen. The virtual form of an eBook reduces your ability to deeply engage with the book mentally, as well as physically.

A hard print of a book is something you can keep forever. You can lend it to friends, family, or even give it to your future children. Even if you do decide to read primarily in eBook form, it's always a great idea to consider getting physical copies of your very favorite stories to own.

And on the note of sharing books, physical copies allow you and others to annotate. Annotating is a very special way of making a story your own through your interpretation, or someone else's by reading their annotations. By writing directly on the page of a purchased copy (please don't annotate library books), you can make sense of the words, highlight quotes, write notes in the margins, and tab favorite passages. This is a special concept that you can use to share literature with others—you could trade a book with a friend, partner, or family member, each of you reading the other's and adding your own annotations. Sometimes in secondhand bookshops you'll stumble across a book that has been annotated by a stranger (some even have separate sections for annotated literature). This is a unique way to glimpse other people's thoughts while leaving your own, and annotation is an opportunity that only physical copies afford.

Hard copies are also much more commonly romanticized than eBooks. I mean, can you imagine Belle or Hermione reading from a Kindle? The gentle paper smell and physical beauty of a book are irreplicable. You can even display books in a small personal library, in your room, or around your home. If you don't like the cover of a treasured book, there's plenty of services out there for custom-illustrated covers that you can slide onto your personal copy. Many popular authors also offer special edition copies that often have especially prized cover design.

...

Despite the timeless attributes of hard copies, though, eBooks also deserve their time in the limelight. A part of the movement of comfort that modern technology allows, they allow you to read almost anywhere, anytime, with unlimited content. Like most other creations that are technology-related, convenience, efficiency, and versatility are the key attributes of an eBook.

When reading virtually, you won't have to deal with the physical bulk or fragility of a hard copy. This might be an easier transition into reading for fun, because you won't have to go out and get a book, nor carry it around. An eBook can go wherever your device goes, so there won't be any forgetting your book at home. Plus, no one will be able to tell what you're reading (or even if you're reading at all) when you're simply staring at a screen, if that's important to you.

You might find that reading virtually is particularly appealing if you're unwilling to make a trip to a library or bookstore, or if there isn't one close by. There's no need to search in multiple locations for a title you're looking for, because you can access any book you want from the comfort of your room with a few clicks. There are also times when the nearest libraries and bookstores have sold out of a particular book, or all copies have been checked out. This often happens with new releases or recently popular titles, and the annoyance of not being able to access a book is eliminated with eBooks. When you buy an online copy, you won't have to wait in line or delay your perusal until someone else has returned the book.

Do keep in mind, however, that eBooks can be and sometimes are remotely deleted. This means that even if you've bought a copy and are in the middle of reading it, it might not be there the next day. This doesn't happen often, but if there's a book you want access to for a long time, I wouldn't recommend purchasing it in eBook form.

Another benefit of reading an electronic copy is that it relieves the pressure of taking a trip to a library itself. It can be understandably overwhelming to navigate a building filled to the brim with books. You won't need to physically return or check out anything, and if you're particularly nervous, you won't need to find a physical copy at all. While I do think it's a great experience to visit your local library at least once, skipping a trip completely is always an option. In fact, the majority of large libraries have their own eBook platforms, which will allow you to check out and read literature for free without stepping foot outside your door. Such programs can allow you further convenience. This can be particularly beneficial if you've been checking out reviews late at night and want to begin your story immediately.

If you don't feel any particular desire to romanticize your reading habits, have no space for a clunky book, or couldn't be less bothered with the smell of a paper page, an eBook might be a great option for you.

Virtual reading can serve as a great transition as you begin to read for fun. And, of course, you'll never have to choose solely one or the other. Again, this journey is all about you. Whenever you feel like reading a physical copy, do it. If you get tired of it? Try an eBook. Every option has its benefits and drawbacks, and it's all about what works for you.

AUDIOBOOKS

Beyond eBooks and hard copies, another way you can "read" is by audiobook. Now, listening to a book *technically* isn't reading. But it does carry many of the same characteristics. For most of this book we've only discussed reading in visual terms—physical, hard copies of printed words on real pages (or screens). But your reading journey has the power to adapt even further. We're lucky enough to live in a world where the advantages of reading can be accessed without even laying eyes on words.

Consider the audiobook. The literary implementation of the technical revolution, audiobooks enable us to read while doing countless other activities. It's the final word in multitasking. It's as easy as listening to a podcast, but instead of commentary, you're immersed in a story. Listening to, rather than physically reading, a book enables you to do anything that doesn't require your ears to complete. It could even serve as a substitute for music or podcasts. Hikes, chores, car rides? An audiobook might be the compromise you've needed between literature and time conservation.

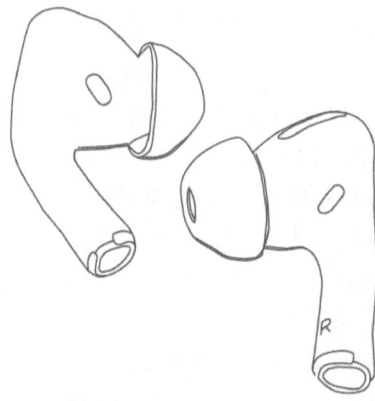

Sounds perfect, right? But like most things in our modern world, convenience does come with its drawbacks. By taking away the actual "reading" factor from your reading, you'll limit the increase in WPM and eye-to-brain comprehension that physical books can give you. Maybe the time saved between multitasking chores while reading is a fair enough trade-off for a faster reading speed, but do keep in mind that this also means work, or school, readings won't become as effortless as they might have through visual perusal (although you may end up choosing to do *ugh* reading itself through audiobook form). Don't forget that listening to a story may take you many times longer to complete than physically reading it—the pace of your consumption hinges on the audiobook narrator's speed. Of course, this depends on how fast you normally read and the length of the book, but it is also difficult to fully engage with a story when it's only your hearing that is immersed.

Don't let these drawbacks discourage you, though. They speak more to the advantages of physical novels than the disadvantages of audiobooks. Because you're still hearing the book, you're still being actively exposed to a unique writing style and vocabulary. Listening to audiobooks also has the benefit of the narrator's inflection. This ties in with that broadened vocab: you'll learn exactly how to pronounce those unfamiliar words while they're in context. It can also improve language command, so while you're not necessarily improving your reading ability, you'll still be picking up speaking and listening skills. This might be particularly beneficial to those unfamiliar with a particular language—audiobooks can serve as a great stepping stone to fluency.

An internet connection is all you need to access thousands of worlds, tales, and adventures. There are several apps you can download for mobile devices, and many share a platform with eBooks. But before purchasing subscriptions, do be sure to check and see if your library offers a free audiobook database, like Overdrive. When it comes to apps, nearly every big streaming or development service offers their own version of an audiobook library. There are often offers for free trials, so be sure to take advantage of those, too.

It all comes down to what works for you. What do you have time for? What do you want to gain from reading? Although hard copies are classic, it's very possible that audiobooks might be what allows you to finally get into reading for fun.

CHAPTER 6

Romanticization

NOW YOU KNOW PRACTICALLY ALL THERE IS to it. How to read for fun: why to do it, when to do it, where to find books, and what to read. But there's a piece to literature that we've overlooked so far, a piece that I think is just as important as your ability to read through the pages. To truly connect to your reading, you'll need to feel the pull of the action itself. What exactly is it that makes reading so different? It can become a positive part of your life, a part that makes your life feel fuller. Glamorize your reading and turn it into something that makes you feel like you're on your way to becoming exactly who you want to be—romanticize it.

Until now we've thought of reading as an activity. Romanticization makes it an *experience*. Consider all the book-loving characters that have reached worldwide fame (think Belle, Hermione, Matilda). Book lovers are almost guaranteed to be the protagonist in any story, and for good reason. Being able to define yourself as a reader gives you an almost "magical" quality—you've unlocked the ability to travel to any world you desire through the mere pages in your hands. We want to harness that magical quality and apply it to the *way* that you read. Doing so can make it just that much more engaging. It'll help you connect better with the words themselves, feel more satisfied with your progress, and encourage you to read more.

...

I have this memory of myself when I was about four years old. This was during the era when I'd wear princess dresses to preschool. I'd don a different special getup each week, and my mom would have to convince me out of wearing the tiaras and sparkly flats to school, too. I was *obsessed* with all things Disney, especially Tinker Bell and Belle.

A lot from that age is obviously hazy, if not completely gone, but I have a distinct memory of sitting on the living room couch in my old house and watching *Beauty and the Beast* on our boxy TV. I've always been relatively short, but at that point my legs were small enough that I could fully extend them and still not have them hang off the end of the couch seat. My mom had wrapped a pink, fuzzy blanket around me, and tucked my stuffed rabbit under my arm. (Yes, I'm an only child.) So I sat there, content and warm with my mom as we watched the story of Belle and the cursed prince unfold.

Belle has always been my favorite princess. Tinker Bell would have given her a run for her money (because she could fly and had magic powers), but as a fairy she technically wasn't a princess. Even at that age, I loved books. At one year old, even though I couldn't yet read, I'd memorized *The Very Hungry Caterpillar* and *Brown Bear, Brown Bear, What Do You See?* in their entireties, solely because I'd begged my parents to read them to me so many times. Yet even after every story I'd read, every character I'd met, and every adventure I'd been on, Belle's story still stood out to me. She was the "it" girl. I wanted to BE her. My mom tells me I wouldn't take off my Belle dress for days.

If you think about it, Belle's character is nearly the epitome of romanticization. Her story takes something as awful as kidnapping and turns it into a swoon-worthy tale of love. We can do a similar thing (albeit much less extreme). Take reading, something that you might currently consider drab, and beautify it. It's as easy as taking a normal breakfast, putting it on a pretty plate, and immediately making it twice as desirable. Take the fact that you've decided to read for fun, stick it in a pleasing frame, and watch as you start to want to read more.

What romanticization means to you will be different from what it means to me, just like how beauty means something different to everyone. Maybe it means that you listen to piano music while you curl up on your couch with a novel. Maybe you'd prefer to be surrounded by people and enjoy the idea of entering your own world amidst so many others. The reason this works is that it helps shape your life into the aesthetic you want it to be. If you're reading this book, you're attempting to make reading a part of your life. But have you envisioned your life with reading in it? Where are you? What color is the cover? Are you laying down or sitting up? If you envision and idealize this image before you make it a reality, it'll be far easier to convert it to physical existence.

Romanticization, like anything else, isn't a cure-all. Glamorizing the small bits of life may sound ridiculous to some of you—you'd rather cut right to the chase. Who has the time to make reading feel *pretty*? While it may be something you scoff at now, don't be afraid to give it a shot. Life is beautiful, and reading can make it more so (if you let it).

I've created a few scenarios with the hope that they'll get you started on envisioning what your reading will look like (and yes, maybe I wanted to have a little fun with it too). There's just something so aesthetic about sitting and being totally immersed in a book. As you read, remember that romanticization will look and feel different from person to person and day to day. Now, these scenes all pertain to the physical copy of a book, simply because they're what most people envision when they picture the act of reading. If you can't imagine yourself in any similar situations, try to extend the pattern to your personal routine. Romanticization means taking the ordinary and making it appealing through the way you look at it. With luck, these short scenes will help get you started on shaping your experiences:

HOW TO READ FOR FUN 89

Catcher in the Rye by J. D. Salinger

It's an overcast day in the bustling city, and the other commuters have their chins tucked into their coats and their hands in their pockets as they walk—they're almost buzzing with purpose. The old-cigarette smell that unfailingly clings to the corners of these blocks has been dampened by the moisture, replaced by the crisp tang of cold air. Your work for the day is done, and while seeking refuge from the chill you spot the warm glow of the café just across the street. Perfect—you'd kill for a hot drink. The bell tinkles as you nudge open the glass door with your shoulder (it's much too cold to take a hand out of your pocket), and the rich scent of coffee pricks at your stiff face. After a quick exchange at the counter, you find yourself settling down in a lounge chair deep within the cafe with a chocolate croissant and a steaming mocha. Typically, you'd opt for a window bar-seat, but the cold has managed to compromise even the nearest proximity to the glass. As you take off your coat and snuggle into the chair, your copy of Holden's story warms your lap. You open the cover and his world washes over you as melting cocoa sweetens your tongue.

Uglies by Scott Westerfeld

Glimmering light sifts through the window and hits the side of the coffee table, the brown carpet, rendering them almost golden. The light refracts off a chiseled glass centerpiece on the table, creating a thousand shimmering rays around the room, warming the space.

You've turned on your Bluetooth speaker so it gently plays piano covers of 2010's classics, filling the bright room with melody. It's a blissfully quiet day, one of those rare spring mornings when everything is so busy blooming that it leaves no space for heat, cold, or anxiety. It's rare for you to feel like this—the morning has positively brimming with possibility and positivity. This is the kind of moment that makes your eyes turn up and your lips curl unconsciously, the kind that makes your heart smile and your soul soar. Even the light is on your side. Lounging back on the armrest of your sofa and stretching your feet out in front of you, you prop a pillow into your lap. The speaker now plays a gentle rendition of One Direction's "If I Could Fly," and you tap your feet to the rhythm as you wedge your hand between the couch cushions, reaching for your copy of *Uglies*. You note with satisfaction that the paperback's white cover is a nearly exact match with the color the wall has turned in the spaces the sun now graces. The oddly smooth feel of the pages of the book as you run them across your right thumb intrigues you. You do it again. Finally opening the book to where you've stuck a folded tissue to mark your place, you wiggle into the couch cushions and return to Tally's operation room.

Crazy Rich Asians by Kevin Kwan

Anger sluices through your veins, frustration grinding around your brain. Nothing's gone right today, this week, this *month*. There's nothing you can do about it but you're tired, exasperated with the audacity of life as it throws you difficulty after difficulty after difficulty. Storming into the living room, you spy *Crazy Rich Asians* splayed open, face down on the couch. Sudden hatred spikes through you. Not even the book could close properly? The way it's just calmly laying there… atrocious. The urge to throw things spikes through you, sending your fingers twitching as you contemplate the absurdity of being angry at a book. Suddenly put out and drained, you flop, stomach-down, onto the stiff couch and smush a pillow over your head. Peering out of one eye at the spine of the novel, the lure of plush couches and fantastical parties dampens your thoughts. *How easy they have it*, you think, *to be born into such luxury*. Squishing your head back towards the couch cushion, you reach out for the book's creased spine. At least the bent cover makes it easier to hold open. Wiggling around a bit gets your back under you and the pages above, and you decide that the day has been hectic enough that you deserve a break. Indulging your tired muscles, you sink a little deeper into the couch and resume the chapter the book had been left on.

Nine by Zach Hines

Your eyes fall closed. *Crash*. Again and again until it fades in and you can almost see the shape of the wave with your ears as it beats against the shore. There's not much song to it, you think, but there's been so much sung, spoken, lyricized, about the sound of waves that it's impossible to simply write it off. Today's a humid but warm day, a kind comparison to the scalding heat of the past week. Settling down with your towel on a nice patch of beach, you shake off your sand-covered volume of *Nine*. It's had just the right amount of tension, violence, and mystery to keep you hooked thus far. Splayed under the sapphire sky, your muscles are practically melting, your skin feels just the right side of sun-kissed, and you can practically feel tension leaving with the rivulets of sweat down your neck. You've considered re-watching *Gossip Girls* (Season 4 of course), but it felt wrong to have earbuds in in the presence of the crashing waves. It also hadn't been worth the effort to squint into a screen against the gleaming sunlight. Nestling into the sand, you pick apart the book where you've found your dog-eared page from yesterday. Sighing deeply, eyes half-lidded, it's all too easy to sink back into the story as the beach molds to your body.

Flipped by Wendelin Van Draanen

The subway smells particularly grimy today, and even the aluminum walls seem to reek of must. The light overhead is overly bright, the fluorescents creating stark shadows on the faces of other passengers. Despite the unwelcoming transportation, today's been an exceptional day. You woke up without bleary eyes for the first time all month, and it's made your back straighter, work faster, and coffee sweeter. Bored with the screech of the subway on its power line, you reach for the tiny volume resting beside your seat. The copy of *Flipped* that you found waiting inconspicuously on the shelf of the secondhand bookstore feels unfamiliar, its worn, browned pages softer than the library books you're used to. You flip open the tattered cover, and soon you're whisked away to the story of Bryce and Juli— two awkward young neighbors who might just never realize they're both right for each other. The two have just met for the first time when the metro speakers *ding* and you scramble to gather your things as you dash off the subway.

The Hunger Games by Suzanne Collins

A running leap into bed has you sprawled on the thick duvet, aching from the stiffness of a long day. You roll your hips over and your back pops one, two, three times as a sigh escapes you. After laying helplessly on your back and staring at the ceiling for a minute or two, you begin to crave the story you'd left off—does Katniss manage to save Peeta? Where does empathy end and survival instinct take over? Blindly reaching over to your nightstand, you grope around until you feel the familiar shape of the paperback and grab it. Body melting into the mattress, face buried against a pillow that smells of home, you hear the boom of the death cannon as you re-enter the Hunger Games.

...

Many of these scenarios are typically taken as thoroughly ordinary. Riding a subway, lying in bed, getting coffee…with or without their relation to reading, these are all generally mundane tasks. But romanticization can give those actions throughout your day an enhanced quality of *more*. If you ever find yourself becoming disenchanted with a book or any other literature, try appealing to the action of reading itself. Creating these kinds of scenarios in real life can help get you more excited about your literature and make it something that feels more like an experience than a task—a process that will ultimately make you a better, and more willing, reader.

If you ever find yourself falling out of love with reading or need help falling in love with it in the first place, romanticize it. The goal is to help literature become a part of your life in a way that makes it more beautiful.

...

You've now been armed with the skills, knowledge, and hopefully the motivation it will take to go out and find *the* book—the one that changes everything.

Language has immense power: it can shape mindsets, create universes, and inspire great action. But more importantly, it can make life more enjoyable. It can make *your* life more enjoyable. Good luck, and happy reading!

Referenced Literature

Beowulf by Unknown

An epic poem originally written in Old English that has found its way into many classrooms' curriculum. It's a legend that tells the tale of the hero Beowulf against the monster Grendel (it also includes a dragon who guards a hoard of treasure). The poem has been adapted to film.

Brown Bear, Brown Bear, What Do You See? by Bill Martin Jr.

A very popular children's book that many (myself included) adored as a baby. Vibrantly illustrated, riddled with rhymes, and filled with different animals, it has helped many youngsters learn to read for fun.

Catcher in the Rye by J. D. Salinger

> Overused by English teachers but deceptively funny, this novel is known by students across the nation. The story features main character Holden Caulfield, a cynical and sarcastic boy whose relatability makes him loveable. The novel follows Holden's expulsion from prep school and his aimless adventures through New York City.

Crazy Rich Asians by Kevin Kwan

> A dazzling satirical comedy about the lives of the filthy rich—and one unsuspecting girl, as she's thrust into her boyfriend's world of old money, new money, and social politics. It's part of a series and has a very popular film adaptation.

Diary of a Wimpy Kid series by Jeff Kinney

> A universally appreciated series that details the life of the awkward, lazy Greg Heffley in lighthearted diary entries and fun illustrations. Nearly every school-age child has heard of these books. It's filled with easy laughs and relatable characters—and has several film adaptations.

Divergent by Veronica Roth

> This novel is set in a dystopian world that is split into five factions that each uphold a different value (selflessness, intelligence, honesty, kindness, or bravery). Romance meets thriller in this personal

favorite. *Divergent* is part of a trilogy and the series has been adapted to film.

Flipped by Wendelin Van Draanen

Known for its movie adaptation but even better in book form, *Flipped* is a romantic comedy that captures the clumsy naivete of a first crush. Told from two perspectives, we're taken on the journey of two young neighbors who can never seem to love each other at the same time.

Geronimo Stilton series by Elisabetta Dami

A best-selling children's book series that details the life of Geronimo Stilton, a nervous and polite mouse who's always getting caught up in the adventures of his friends and family.

Harry Potter series by J. K. Rowling

These are the fantasy books that everyone knows. This series follows Harry Potter, a charming and determined young boy who has been living a miserable life with his selfish aunt and uncle. He's thrust into the magical world when he discovers that he himself is a wizard and gladly goes to live at renowned magical school, Hogwarts—a place of fantastical possibility and adventure. The complexity and endearing charm of such a captivating world has earned the series global recognition, an enormous fan base, and a widely-loved series of film adaptations.

Junie B. Jones series by Barbara Park

> A popular children's series that follows the adventures of sassy kindergartener Junie B. Jones with a lighthearted charm. The books have been adapted into a series of musicals.

Little Women by Louisa May Alcott

> A beloved coming-of-age novel that tells the story of four sisters (Meg, Jo, Beth, and Amy) on their journey to womanhood. Alcott's classic speaks of adventure and love in an affectionate tale that has several popular film adaptations.

Lord of the Flies by William Golding

> Commonly included in Language Arts curriculum nationwide, Golding's novel depicts several children stranded on an island and allows human nature to run its course. The book's distinctive characters, intense action, and haunting reflection of humanity have made it a globally recognized title. It also has a film adaptation.

Magic Tree House series by Mary Osborn

> This popular series follows Jack and Annie, two young siblings who have discovered a tree house whose magic books can take them to periods throughout history. Their exciting adventures have made *Magic Tree House* an easily recognizable name, particularly amongst elementary-age children.

Nine by Zach Hines

> This is a clever twist on the typical teen dystopian story. In this world, everyone has nine lives to live, and they're encouraged to burn through them (glamorized suicide) by the government, who's implemented incentives for death with the goal of controlling overpopulation.

Nineteen Eighty-four by George Orwell

> This novel is a cautionary tale that high school English teachers love to use as a reflection on media regulation, manipulation, and the power of government. This book takes place in an imagined future where the world is ruled by The Party and independent thinking is actively persecuted by the "Thought Police." It's the birthplace of the term "Big Brother," and has become the literary original of a political dystopia.

Of Mice and Men by John Steinbeck

> A short but meaningful novella that narrates the journey of two destitute laborers, George and Lennie, on their search for work across California. Known for its contrasting characters, straightforward prose and startling ending, this is another classroom staple.

Pride and Prejudice by Jane Austen

> One of the most well-known classics of all time,

and touted to be the "original enemies to lovers" story, *Pride and Prejudice* is a title every reader knows. The story follows Elizabeth Bennet and her sisters as they navigate love, family reputation, and social standing. The novel has been adapted to film several times.

Rainbow Magic series by Daisy Meadows, Narinder Dhami, Linda Chapman, Lucy Diamond, Karen Ball, & Marilyn Kaye

A series of dozens of short books that are each about a special fairy, such as *Ruby the Red Fairy* or *Sky the Blue Fairy,* and their adventures throughout Fairyland. The series is immensely popular among young girls worldwide.

Rich Dad, Poor Dad by Robert Kiyosaki with Sharon Lechter

An insightful book that teaches its readers how to get rich and *stay* rich. A well-known title because of its uniqueness, it details how to escape the "rat race" and become successful—and how to teach your kids to do so as well.

Sapiens: A Brief History of Humankind by Yuval Noah Harari

A highly acclaimed volume that takes its readers through humankind's history, from our prehistoric roots to our ultimate domination of the world.

Harari discusses the human as a species through our Cognitive Revolution, Agricultural Revolution, unification, and the Scientific Revolution. It is a transformative book that reflects on the existence of humankind through a scientific lens.

The 48 Laws of Power by Robert Greene

"For those who want power, watch power, or want to arm themselves against power," this book is a bold collection of the laws of ultimate control. Drawn from history, philosophy, and cunning analysis, the bestseller quickly gained popularity amidst a wave of demand for books that revolutionize independent thinking and nonconformity.

The Grapes of Wrath by John Steinbeck

A classic that details the journey of one American family across the midwest in search of "the promised land," it reflects the migration of thousands during the Great Depression. It's a heavily discussed classroom text because of its enduring themes and historical context, and was adapted to film in 1940.

The Great Gatsby by F. Scott Fitzgerald

Arguably the most recognizable name in literature, this book is known for its subtle critique of the dazzling party culture it details, as well as its atypical rejection of the American Dream. It is one of those rare titles that are often beloved by teacher and student alike and has been adapted to film multiple times.

The Hate U Give by Angie Thomas

A fearlessly authentic novel that tells the story of Starr, the only witness to the death of her unarmed best friend Khalil—at the hands of police. The novel was inspired by the Black Lives Matter movement and has been succeeded by a critically acclaimed film.

The Hunger Games by Suzanne Collins

Possibly the most well-known and well-loved dystopian series in existence today, *The Hunger Games* fuses rebellion, survival, and romance into one explosive story. The nation is led by the vibrant and garish Capitol, which lies adjacent to its twelve districts, all in varying states of poverty. Each year, one girl and one boy from each district are selected to compete in the Hunger Games—a fight to the death with only one survivor. The series has been adapted into four very well-received films.

The Other Wes Moore by Wes Moore

This eye-opening memoir discusses social justice through the eyes of two different boys—both of whom are named Wes Moore. Moore tells the true tale of two eerily similar lives that resulted in

HOW TO READ FOR FUN

dramatically different outcomes while examining where such a discrepancy might have begun. Although there is no film adaptation, Moore has made appearances on various programs to discuss his novel.

The Notebook by Nicholas Sparks

Although the name is linked more often with its 2004 movie hit, *The Notebook* embodies the definition of a classic romance novel. The heartbreaking story of Allie and Noah is set in the vibrant period after World War II in North Carolina and often produces tears of both joy and despair. Popular and recognized throughout the nation, the book is a "Great American Read."

The Very Hungry Caterpillar by Eric Carle

A uniquely illustrated and globally popular children's book that has a place in many toddlers' hearts. The story follows the very hungry caterpillar as he eats more and more on his journey to becoming a beautiful butterfly.

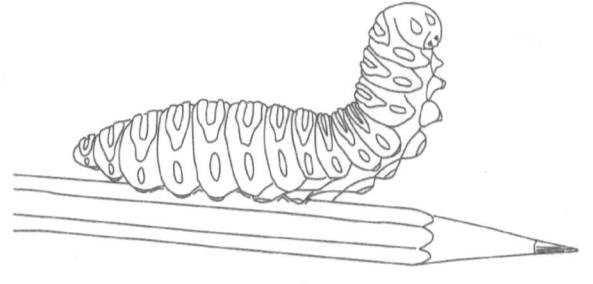

Twilight by Stephenie Meyer

> Known for its steamy romance and charismatic vampires, this series took the world by storm then gained a reputation as a guilty pleasure. The saga has been adapted into several globally appreciated movies.

Uglies by Scott Westerfeld

> Westerfeld's award-winning sci-fi novel depicts a world where everyone is considered "ugly"—until they receive mandated, drastic plastic surgery once they reach the age of sixteen. "Pretties" party their lives away in a paradise city constructed just for them, but the other side isn't so glamorous. Engaging and thoughtful, this book grew very popular upon release and has been continued through a trilogy.

World War Z by Max Brooks

> A popular book that tells the story of our world after it has been ravaged by the Zombie War through several different perspectives. Brooks speaks on humanity's survival in terms of economy, politics, culture, and environment in a hauntingly gripping work. It has a movie adaptation, although it is said to be dissimilar to the book.

Zodiac by Robert Graysmith

> A renowned true crime work that follows the

unsolved murders committed by the "Zodiac Killer," a serial killer who claimed thirty-seven lives. It has been adapted into a mystery thriller film.

Resources

Abbate, Bill. "How to Use Deadlines to Your Advantage." *Medium*, February 5, 2022, https://medium.com/illumination-curated/how-to-use-deadlines-to-your-advantage-d3d6f717128e.

"Benefits of Reading: Why You Should Read More." *JRE Library*, 11 Dec. 2017, https://jrelibrary.com/articles/benefits-of-reading-why-you-should-read-more/.

"Book Clubs." *Fable.co*, https://fable.co/book-clubs.

"Coping With a Book Hangover - Goodreads News & Interviews." *Goodreads*, Goodreads, June 24, 2018, https://www.goodreads.com/blog/show/1304-13-ways-of-coping-with-a-book-hangover.

Franzen, Mara. "How to Romanticize Your Reading Life." *BOOK RIOT*, November 10, 2021, https://bookriot.com/romanticize-your-reading-life/.

Gerwig, Greta, director. *Little Women*. December 7, 2019, Sony Pictures Entertainment.

"How Students Benefit from Learning with Ebooks." *South University*, October 18, 2013, https://www.

southuniversity.edu/news-and-blogs/2013/10/how-students-benefit-from-learning-with-ebooks.

Latourrette, Christopher, and Morgan Haas. "To Read or Not to Read; That is the Question." *VCU Undergraduate Research Posters*, 2020.

Martinez, Karina Mercedes. "How to Read for Fun—Seven Tips for Getting Started," *New Forum*, UC Irvine, August 21, 2021, https://sites.uci.edu/newforum/2019/08/23/how-to-read-for-fun-seven-tips-for-getting-started/.

Prose, Francine, et al. "I Know Why the Caged Bird Cannot Read." *Harper's Magazine* , September 1, 1999, https://harpers.org/archive/1999/09/i-know-why-the-caged-bird-cannot-read/.

Rayner, Keith, et al. "So Much to Read, so Little Time." *Psychological Science in the Public Interest*, vol. 17, no. 1, 2016, pp. 4–34., https://doi.org/10.1177/1529100615623267.

Seifert, Christine. "The Case for Reading Fiction." *Harvard Business Review*, May 28, 2020, https://hbr.org/2020/03/the-case-for-reading-fiction.

Sharma, Subodh. "Audiobooks." *GladReaders*, January 1, 2022, https://gladreaders.com/benefits-of-audiobooks/.

Sleep Advisor. "Reading Before Bed." *Sleep Advisor*, October 12, 2021, https://www.sleepadvisor.org/reading-before-bed/.

"Specific Application Questions." *Columbia University*, https://undergrad.admissions.columbia.edu/apply/process/columbia-questions.

Acknowledgments

First of all, if you're reading this it means that you have taken the time to read through my very first publication, and that means more to me than words can express. Thank you to every reader.

I owe a very special thanks to Sallie Vandagrift, my editor, Melissa Thomas, my designer, and my project manager, Kim Harper-Kennedy, as well as the entire brilliant team at Luminare, to whom I can accredit the very existence of this book. I am also indebted to James Chott, whose talent made the illustrations in this book come to life. Thank you all for your patience, support, and meticulous work.

Next, I have to mention my parents, who have allowed me the opportunity to follow my passions. Thank you, Dad, for working tirelessly to enable, motivate, and inspire me, and thank you, Mom, for pushing me to grow and always look ahead. Where would I be without that one dinner that sparked this project in the first place? And to my wonderful friends—thank you for your endless love and encouragement.

Finally, thank you to the incredible authors that pour their hearts into their craft and write literature that is irresistible. Without your work this book would not have been possible.

www.ingramcontent.com/pod-product-compliance
Lightning Source LLC
LaVergne TN
LVHW092052060526
838201LV00047B/1349